Employer Engagement Toolkit

A step-by-step guide to building strong and sustainable
business/education partnerships for CTE, STEM, and Academy leaders

Brett Pawlowski • Charlie Katz

Columbia, MD • www.NC3T.com

About The National Center for College and Career Transitions
The National Center for College and Career Transitions, or NC3T, has
a twofold mission: "Every Teen with a Dream and a Plan, and Every
Community with a Capable, Ready Workforce." The organization
works to connect schools, postsecondary institutions, and
employers in order to introduce students to the array of options
available to them, and to help them prepare for the types of
opportunities for which they are best suited. For more information,
visit www.NC3T.com.

Table of Contents

Section IV. Measuring Partnership Outcomes

Section V. Engaging Partners for the Long Haul

Section VI. Deep Dive: Advisory Boards

Section VII. EET Case Studies

Section I

Partnership Essentials

1.1 Why Do Businesses and Schools Need Each Other?

Businesses have been involved in education since the beginning of public schooling in the United States. In fact, if it weren't for the business community, public schools might not have started when they did: After legislators in Massachusetts denied Horace Mann's appeal for a free and public system, he turned to the business community for help, and their appeals — based on their interests in workforce preparedness — convinced lawmakers to act. Business leaders were also instrumental in creating the vocational education system in the 1920s as work became more specialized.

However, while business/education partnerships continue to be strong in some areas (particularly in many Career and Technical Education, or CTE, programs), we have witnessed a growing disconnect between businesses and schools over the past few decades. Too often, businesspeople aren't sure how to get involved or how to make a meaningful contribution, while educators feel that they are responsible for meeting so many mandates that partnership work remains in the "should do" pile rather than the "must do" pile.

So in the big picture, why is it so important for businesses and schools to work together? And why is the need particularly urgent now?

Retiring Baby boomers: A Game Changer

You wouldn't think about retirees having much of an impact on schools. But as the Baby boomers retire, they will cause seismic changes in both business and education. The chart below shows the scale of the change, with the percentage of Americans at age 65 or older growing at triple the rate of previous years, and

Percentage of US Population aged 65 years or older, 1980–2050

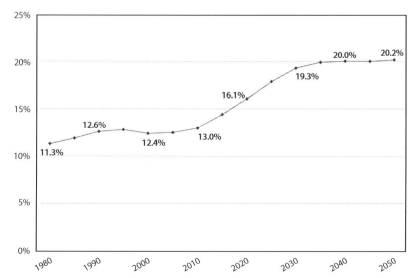

Source: US Census Bureau

in just 20 years — from 2010 to 2030 — the percentage of adults at or above retirement age grows from 13 percent to nearly 20 percent of the US population, an increase from 40 million to 72 million seniors!

This wave of retirements — a tsunami, actually — has tremendous implications for business and for education.

The Big Picture — for Businesses

For the past few decades, the business community's relationship with schools has been mixed. Some businesses have stayed engaged with local CTE programs because they see a direct payoff and connection to their business needs. Many more, however, have been frustrated by a lack of responsiveness from schools to their concerns about graduate quality, and have defaulted to a focus on policy rather than engagement, lobbying on issues such as content standards, charter school authorization, and teacher evaluation.

The economy of the 1950s, 60s, and 70s required a few well-educated managers to call the shots for a large pool of semi-skilled labor. Beginning in the 1980s, the landscape started to shift away from the post-war era economy and toward a new, globally connected economy. With trade barriers falling and dozens of countries entering the free-market economy, and with the rise of anytime-anywhere information technology, the jobs landscape shifted and skills demands rose steadily for US workers. In today's economy, about two-thirds of all jobs require a postsecondary credential or degree, and with that, a higher level of literacy, mathematical reasoning, and agile thinking than ever before.

This shift in the skills needed in today's workforce will be exacerbated by the coming wave of Baby Boomer retirements. Baby boomers were the most highly educated workforce in the world during their generation. But now, the younger US workforce is not nearly as well educated as similarly-aged workers in

How satisfied are you with the job these schools are doing graduating students with skills/ knowledge to succeed in the global economy?

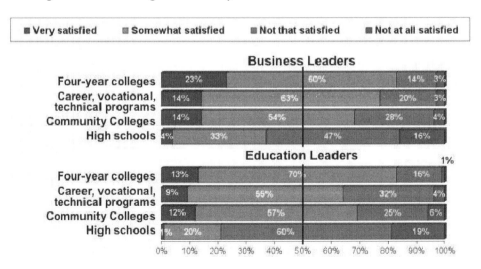

Source: *Across the Great Divide: Perspectives of CEOs and College Presidents on America's Higher Education and Skills Gap*, US Chamber of Commerce, March 2011

Jobs requiring a college degree versus number of college graduates, 2010

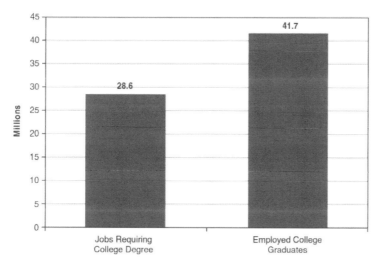

Source: Why Are Recent College Graduates Underemployed?, Center for College Affordability and Productivity, January 2013

competitor nations. The challenge in education lies not in returning to the "good old days," but in anticipating and responding to the ever-increasing skills and knowledge needed for the future.

Businesses, however, continue to see a large percentage of young people as being unprepared for work. Too many students graduate high school and even college unprepared for the realities of the workplace because of their lack of soft skills (interpersonal skills, employability skills, etc.) or practical training.

And our "bachelor's degree for all" mentality has pushed too many into four-year programs, creating an oversupply of young people with bachelor's degrees or higher, and an undersupply with the postsecondary education needed for the middle-skills positions in desperate search of qualified applicants.

Per-pupil expenditures, 1970–2010

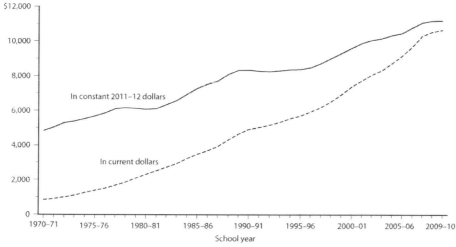

Source: National Center for Education Statistics, US Department of Education

The solution: Bridge the disconnect between businesses and schools, and show students firsthand where the job opportunities are, what kinds of knowledge and skills are required by different careers, what kinds of skills employers expect, and what postsecondary paths are available to them.

The Big Picture — for Schools

Like the business community, schools have looked at partnerships as being "nice to have" rather than something they "have to have." Businesses were lulled into complacency by having access to a deep, STEM-capable labor pool; schools, on the other hand, saw budgets slowly but consistently rise year after year, and failed to see the necessity of pursuing other sources of support.

The financial crisis of 2008 rocked the education world. A great many schools and districts experienced budget cuts due to lower state and local tax revenues, and had to scramble to adjust.

While some thought this would be a temporary challenge (we have dealt with recessions in the past, after all), declining revenues and tight budgets are more likely to be "the new normal." K–12 education, after all, gets 98 percent of its revenues from federal, state, and local governments. What's going to happen to those revenues when 71 million people leave the workforce and stop paying income taxes? What happens to the competition for existing funds as those retirees require more government services like Medicare? What happens as schools continue to deal with increasing costs related to pensions, employee health care, and transportation?

Rather than a temporary bump in the road, the recent financial crisis represented the start of an ongoing resource challenge for our schools. If we want to support students as we have in the past — in fact, if we want to boost student outcomes — we're going to need the support of community partners, and not just in terms of financial resources.

Businesses and Schools Need Each Other

Businesses cannot build a workforce capable of replacing the boomers without the help of the education system, and schools cannot serve students in the way they'd like in the face of declining funding. The evidence is clear: If businesses and schools are going to succeed in the face of these significant challenges, they can only do so by working together.

1.2 What Is a Partnership?

When educators and employers think about business/education partnerships, it's usually with a focus on workforce preparedness for students. Educators benefit from such a partnership because they're better able to help students reach their goals; employers benefit by having a better prepared labor pool.

However, while workforce preparedness is a common focus for many partnerships in CTE, it's not the only possible area of interest; business partners may be more interested in improving the morale of their staff members by giving them an opportunity to volunteer, and educators may be looking at employer engagement to boost graduation rates or student engagement, or even as a way to increase the resources available to teach.

To account for these different kinds of motivations, we offer a broader definition of business/education partnerships:

> *Educators and businesspeople working together toward a shared goal designed to benefit students while at the same time, achieving goals unique to each partner.*

This definition is left broad on purpose: As you'll see throughout this toolkit, business/education partnerships can feature a wide range of motives, resources, partnership models, and desired outcomes.

Elements of a Partnership

To build an effective initiative, a partnership must have the following elements:

◊ **Partners collaborating as equals** – To be partners, the people involved must all have some say in what the partnership does and how it does it. If partners don't have some influence on the work being done, it is unlikely they'll remain as partners for long.

◊ **Shared (or at least complementary) interests or concerns** – The concept of return on investment, or ROI, is one of the most critical for strong and sustainable partnerships. Basically, everyone involved in your work must see some kind of benefit from their participation. This could be long-term or immediate workforce benefits, it could be good publicity, or it could be improved employee morale. This topic will be covered extensively in this toolkit.

◊ **Partners bring something to the table** – The flip side of giving people a voice in the process is that they must contribute something — resources, personnel, expertise, etc. — to the effort. All partners, including the education partners, must have some "skin in the game."

◊ **A way to measure progress or outcomes** – Partners have to define their desired outcomes, and these have to be measured in some way. This can be informal, but larger efforts benefit greatly from having hard data for partners and others to see. It is important to note although different partners may have different desired outcomes, the partnership model should address them all. As an example, a mentoring program might meet a school's desire for lower dropout rates and an employer's desire for improved employee morale.

Self-Assessment:

List your three most important partners below and answer the following questions:

Partner #1: _____

Partner #2: _____

Partner #3: _____

◊ *Have they helped design the programs they participate in?*

◊ *What benefits do they get from being involved?*

◊ *What do they contribute to the work?*

◊ *How do we measure the outcomes that are important to them?*

Note: *It is not enough to say that "all they care about is helping the kids" — you have to consider the benefits to them, either individually or as a company.*

The Partnership Sequence

In education, many people think about developing business partnerships using the following model:

Identify a problem → Design a solution → Find partners

The elements are right, but the sequence is wrong. If you follow the steps above, your business associates have no say in the focus of your work, and no say in how your problem gets solved. All they're there for is to provide resources to put your plan, to solve your problem, into place. This is actually a sponsorship model, not a partnership model.

Of course, there are times when sponsorships are appropriate; but on the whole, they're much less effective at bringing partners to the table, and not very good at keeping them there. Consider the feedback from business coalitions (such as chambers of commerce and workforce boards) in response to to the following question:

Q: How are business coalitions typically involved in the planning process?

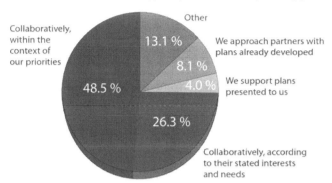

Source: Coalition Leaders Speak Out on Education, DeHavilland Associates, 2007

While individual businesses may respond somewhat differently (we'll cover the difference between businesses and business coalitions later), this graphic indicates that business groups almost never (4 percent) get involved in relationships where a plan is dropped, ready-made, on their desks. They are much more interested in working together with their education partners to create a plan, either centered around the schools' interests (26.3 percent) or around their own (48.5 percent).

There's a second problem with the sponsorship model: You are much more likely to overlook the many ways that your local businesses might support your program. Suppose you decide you need funds for a new computer system, and you approach local businesses asking for donations. With that kind of single-minded approach, you're much more likely to miss out on the other kinds of support they could provide: They may be primed to offer volunteers, mentors, expert support, in-kind donations, or workplace opportunities, but those are unlikely to come up if you lead with such a narrow focus rather than start a conversation.

To move from a sponsorship model to a partnership model, just rearrange the steps outlined above:

Find partners → Identify a problem → Design a solution

By finding partners first, you'll be in a position to identify shared problems, and work together to design a solution that better accounts for the resources available from all partners and leverages the strengths of everyone involved.

Partnership of Equals

Some educators may be hesitant to pursue partnerships because it feels like

"But What About My Needs?"

Much of this toolkit focuses on identifying and focusing on your partners' needs in order to build effective partnerships. As motivational speaker Zig Ziglar said, "You can get everything in life you want if you will just help enough other people get what they want."

But what about your needs? Suppose there are things you really want to put into place, like a career mentoring program? What if your career academy mandates that every student participate in a semester-long internship? Shouldn't you go ask for what you need?

It's fine to highlight your needs as you talk to your partners.

The key is to make it clear that, while you have certain mandates or priorities, your focus is still on working with the needs and resources of your partner.

You could say, "Our career academy requires that every junior participates in an internship in your field, so I'd really like to see if that's a good fit for you. But if it's not — if that doesn't line up with your interests, or if your workplace isn't conducive to that — let's talk about other ideas that would work better for you." This approach makes your needs and priorities clear, but doesn't close the door on other options — options you might not even have thought of — that could benefit your students and staff.

they're begging, asking for donations like a charity. But partnerships are not at all like charities. The key difference: Charities ask for donations to meet the needs of those they serve, with little thought given to how the donor benefits, whereas partners identify areas of shared interest and make a joint investment in ways that provide both parties with concrete returns.

Businesses and others are besieged each day with requests from charities but very few requests from those who understand the advantages and sustainable nature of partnerships. You can either compete with multiple charities for limited resources allocated for donation or enjoy far less competition for a far greater pool of resources with a partnership approach.

The lesson: Understand that in a true partnership, everyone makes a contribution, and everyone receives value. You and your partners are collaborators, working side by side to create something that produces results for everyone involved.

1.3 How Do Partnerships Help Students?

While every stakeholder has to benefit from a partnership for it to be successful (see the Return on Investment discussion in the next section), the primary focus of any business/education engagement has to be on student outcomes.

While contributions of resources (classroom donations, scholarships, and the like) are important, their impact is fairly obvious and will not be addressed here. Instead, this section will focus on what happens when you connect business partners directly with students, such as the issues you can address, and the types of outcomes you can look for.

School/Student Issues That Can Be Addressed Through Partnerships

◊ **Declining Student Engagement**: According to Gallup, student engagement in school declines substantially over time: 76 percent of elementary school students are engaged in school; however, that number drops to 44 percent among high school students. (Gallup)

◊ **Dropping Out**: Fortunately, overall on-time graduation rates have increased to about 80 percent in recent years. Yet each year, approximately 1.3 million students fail to graduate from high school; more than half are students of color. The graduation rate among students of color is as much as 25 percentage points below their white peers. (Alliance for Excellent Education)

◊ **Mediocre International Standing**: American students fare poorly on international comparisons. According to the Organisation for Economic

Student Engagement Over Time, The Gallup Student Poll

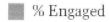 % Engaged

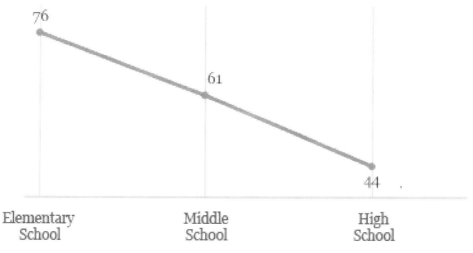

Source: Gallup Student Poll, 2012

Co-operation and Development (OECD), the US spends more on education as a percentage of gross domestic product (GDP) than almost every other country (only five spend more), and yet:

» Among the 34 OECD countries, the United States performed below average in mathematics in 2012 and was ranked 26th. The United States ranked 17th in reading and 21st in science. There has been no significant change in these performances over time.

» Mathematics scores for the top-performer, Shanghai-China, indicate a performance that is the equivalent of more than two years of formal schooling ahead of those observed in Massachusetts, itself a strong-performing state.

» Students in the United States have particular weaknesses in performing mathematics tasks with higher cognitive demands such as translating real-world situations into mathematical terms and interpreting mathematical aspects in real-world problems.

» Despite their below-average performance in mathematics, US students feel relatively confident in their mathematics abilities compared with their counterparts in other countries. For example, 69 percent of US students reported that they felt confident in a mathematical task such as calculating the petrol consumption rate of a car, compared with 56 percent of all OECD students.

◊ **Weak Counseling Opportunities**: Students are not receiving sufficient counseling to prepare for their futures. The recommended ratio of counselors to students is 250:1; the current ratio in schools is 479:1. (CTE's Role in Career Guidance, ACTE, 2008)

How Business Partners Make an Impact

As more schools and districts track student outcomes, research on the impact of effective business engagement is becoming more available. Results to date have been significant, with positive impacts on graduation rates, academic outcomes, student behavior, and post-high school outcomes.

Boosting Graduation Rates

◊ According to a survey of high school dropouts, "Eighty-one percent of survey respondents said that if schools provided opportunities for real-world learning (internships, service learning projects, and other opportunities), it would have improved students' chances of graduating from high school." (The Silent Epidemic, Gates Foundation, 2006)

◊ In 2005, the graduation rate in Nashville was 55 percent; in 2012, after full-scale implementation of the Academies of Nashville model, the graduation rate was 78.4 percent. (Academies of Nashville presentation, 2013) Several other schools and districts implementing a pathways strategy saw similar graduation rate increases of 10 to 15 percent.

Improved Academic/Classroom Outcomes

◊ **Stronger Workplace Skills.** The Linked Learning Alliance reported in 2014 that on its surveys of 11th grade students, the students who participated in a pathways program were:

   » 23 percentage points more likely than comparison students to report that high school prepares them for working with people in professional settings, and for working in groups to achieve a shared goal.

   » 20 percentage points more likely than comparison students to report improved presentation skills.

   » 14 percentage points more likely than comparison students to report improved ability to conduct online searches to answer a question.

   » 12 percentage points more likely than comparison students to report growth in their belief that they could reach their goals with enough effort.

◊ **Increased Student Persistence.** CTE can strongly impact educational persistence, as illustrated by researchers such as Kulik; Grasso and Shea; and Plank, DeLuca and Estacion, who found that a ratio of one CTE course to two academic courses minimized a student's dropout risk. (Career and Technical Education's Role in American Competitiveness, ACTE, 2013)

◊ **Academic Gains and College Preparation.** A 2008 report on students in the California Partnership Academies (Evidence from California Partnership Academies: One Model of Linked Learning Pathways, ConnectEd, 2008) noted academies' impact on outcomes in two areas:

   » 10th graders enrolled in the California Partnership Academies were more likely to pass the California High School Exit Exam than

---

The Impact of Career Connections: Linked Learning, California

Like most schools that rely on an academy or career/college pathways model, California schools participating in Linked Learning have seen early indicators of academic growth. Academic Performance Index (API) scores at the small high schools, for example, have experienced relatively steady increases in base scores between 2008 and 2011.

The implementation of Linked Learning pathways at comprehensive high schools is still in the early stages of development. Of these schools, Hiram W. Johnson has the highest percentage of students enrolled in Linked Learning pathways (69 percent) and has shown marked improvement in several measures of academic achievement in the past three years. Early indicators of improved academic achievement outcomes at Johnson include the following:

• State high school exit exam: A 20 percent increase in 10th grade students passing California state exams in math and English language arts
• Achievement on state test: A 56 percent drop in students scoring "below basic" or "far below basic" on the California Standards Test
• Base API Score increased from 611 in 2008 to 669 in 2011
• Dropout rates decreased 49 percent from 2008-09 to 2010-11

the general state population. On the English Language Arts (ELA) exam, 84 percent of Academy students passed compared with 76 percent of students statewide. On the mathematics exam, 80 percent of Academy students passed, compared with 74 percent statewide.

» Academy students were much more likely to complete the 15 academic courses (the a–g requirements) needed to be eligible for admission to California's public colleges and universities. The study found that 50 percent of graduating seniors in Academies had completed the a–g requirements, compared with 35 percent of graduates statewide.

Addressing Behavior/Social Issues

◊ **Reduced Teen Gang Membership**. In 2005, before instituting the Academies of Nashville, the average age of a gang member in Nashville was 16; in 2012, the average age was 22. (Academies of Nashville presentation, 2013)

◊ **Better Discipline**. Nashville saw a 13 percent decrease in disciple referrals between 2005 and 2012. (Academies of Nashville presentation, 2013)

◊ **Better Attendance**. Attendance in Nashville increased from 89 percent to 93 percent between 2006 and 2012. (Academies of Nashville presentation, 2013)

Improved Student Lifetime Outcomes

◊ **Earnings Gains**. A long-term MDRC study of career academies found that these programs produced substantial earnings gains for participants. Academy students in the study averaged an 11 percent salary increase per year ($2,088). For young men, the increases were significantly higher and totaled almost $30,000 over eight years through a combination of increased wages, hours worked, and employment stability. These earnings increases were achieved after more than 90 percent of the academy students graduated from high school, and the results were most concentrated for at-risk populations that are often difficult to impact. (The Role of Career Academies in Education Improvement, ACTE, 2009)

The Impact of Career Connections: Volusia County Public Schools, Florida

Volusia School District is a suburban/rural district in the county that includes Daytona Beach, Florida. The district runs 36 pathway programs, or career academies, across eight high schools. At present, approximately 28 percent of the student population is enrolled in a career academy; the program's goal is to increase student participation to 35 percent by 2014–15.

Data from the 2009–2010 school year indicates:

- 90 percent graduation rate for career academy students, 78 percent district-wide

- 2.94 unweighted grade point average for career academy students, 2.71 district-wide
- 3.12 grade point average for Advanced Placement/ International Baccalaureate courses for career academy students, 2.86 district-wide
- 30 percent of career academy students had 10 or more absences, 39 percent district-wide
- 30 percent of career academy students had discipline referrals, 49 percent district-wide

Source: Margo Pierce, A Community Affair in Florida, University of Central Florida, May 2012.

◊ A 2004 National Assessment of Vocational Education (NAVE) report showed that students who participated in postsecondary CTE coursework, even without earning credentials, earned a higher yearly salary than high school graduates who did not take postsecondary CTE courses. (CTE: Education for a Strong Economy, ACTE, 2009)

◊ The Career Academies produced sustained earnings gains that averaged 11 percent (or $2,088) more per year for Academy group members than for individuals in the non-Academy group — a $16,704 boost in total earnings over the eight years of follow-up (in 2006 dollars). These labor market impacts were concentrated among young men, a group that has experienced a severe decline in real earnings in recent years. Through a combination of increased wages, hours worked, and employment stability, real earnings for young men in the Academy group increased by $3,731 (17 percent) per year — or nearly $30,000 over eight years. (Career Academies: Long-Term Impacts on Labor Market Outcomes, Educational Attainment, and Transitions to Adulthood, MDRC, 2008)

◊ **Increased Student Motivation and Better Decision-making**. In 2010, an organization in the United Kingdom compiled a summary of the research on the ways in which students benefit from working with employers (What Is to Be Gained through Partnership, 2010; Education and Employers Taskforce). They found evidence of the following impacts:

» There is evidence to show that employer engagement typically makes learning more enjoyable and interesting for young people. A 2008 survey of young people who had recently completed a work placement showed that 49 percent found it "very enjoyable" with a further 31 percent calling their experience "mostly enjoyable."

» Professor Andrew Miller's in-depth investigation of the impact of business mentoring found that the "majority of students said that mentoring has affected their wish to do well at school. Three quarters of these said that mentoring has had a lot of impact on their motivation in General Certificate of Secondary Education (GCSE) subjects." In addition, the best engagements of employers have "significantly enhanced" pupil "learning and enthusiasm for the subject" of study.

» A 2010 survey by KPMG of 151 primary and secondary school leaders indicated that 75 percent of respondents agreed or strongly agreed that involvement of employers in pupil learning specifically has a positive impact on attainment.

» A series of studies in the United Kingdom indicate that there is evidence to show those young people who have had the most chance to interact with employers at school are better placed to make informed and confident choices about future careers.

»   Evidence suggests that there is an important link between employer engagement in education and ultimate social mobility.

◊   **Ability to Live Independently**. Career Academies produced an increase in the percentage of young people living independently with children and a spouse or partner. Young men also experienced positive impacts on marriage and being custodial parents. (Career Academies: Long-Term Impacts on Labor Market Outcomes, Educational Attainment, and Transitions to Adulthood, MDRC, 2008)

◊   **Academic and Earnings Benefits**. According to the latest research from the National Academies Foundation (NAF), students attending Academies saw the following outcomes:

»   52 percent of NAF graduates earn bachelor's degrees in four years compared with 32 percent nationally.

»   Of those who go on to post-secondary education, more than 50 percent are the first in their families to attend college.

»   90 percent of students report that the Academies helped them to develop career plans.

»   85 percent of five- and 10-year alumni are working in a professional field.

»   Career academy graduates sustained $16,704 (11 percent) more in total earnings over the eight years following high school than non-Academy group members who were also studied.

It is clear that there are many different ways in which business partners can impact the lives of students, depending on the partnership model and the goals that you set.

1.4 Return on Investment (ROI): The Foundation of Successful Partnerships

One of the most important concepts in creating and maintaining strong and sustainable partnerships is Return On Investment, or ROI.

Everyone involved in your partnerships — including you and your business partners, but also your administrators, students, and parents — has to contribute something to make your partnership possible. Administrators have to approve expenditures or use of facilities; parents have to sign approval slips, and possibly bear additional costs or do extra driving to allow students to participate.

For these people to contribute to your partnership — and especially for them to be willing to stay for the long haul — they need to get something back. They have lots of things they could be doing with their time, attention, money, or other resources: Why would they give them to you?

They need a return on their investment in your program.

Thinking in terms of ROI is empowering. When you realize that people have options, you can think about how your program can offer a greater benefit than the alternatives available to them. Once you've identified benefits that you can offer that will be attractive to them, you're well on your way to building a partnership with great promise and real momentum.

Look at the Stakeholder Chart sample below to get a sense of how a partnership program might appeal to different stakeholders, then use the chart on the next page as a template for your program design work.

Sample Stakeholder Chart for a Career Mentoring Program			
Stakeholder	**Role**	**Need from Them**	**Provide to Them**
Students	Participant	Participation and completion	Opportunity to explore career of interest
Parents	Student Support	Allow child to participate; sign permission slip; drive student	Promise of career exploration, better direction for future
Co. Management	Host program	Use of facilities; approval of staff participation	Employee morale, promise of stronger future workforce
Co. Employees	Act as mentors	Time, training, commitment	Rewarding feeling, improved job satisfaction
School Admin.	Host program	Background checks; approve staff and student participation	Promise of improved student performance and retention

artnership Planning Worksheet: Stakeholder Chart

Use this template to identify all of the likely stakeholders for your partnership programs and consider the role they will play, what you need them to do, and what return they will realize from their investment.

Stakeholder	Role	Need from Them	Provide to Them
Students			
Parents			
Teachers			
School Administrators			
School Board/ District Leaders			
Company Management			
Company Employees			
Company Customers			

1.5 How Businesses Benefit from Partnerships

The US Chamber of Commerce estimates that the business community contributes close to $4 billion each year to K–12 education. And much of that support goes to CTE programs, in the form of financial support, donated goods and services, and most importantly, the time of professionals who work with students, staff, and administrators.

If you were to ask most CTE teachers, they would say that their business partners are involved primarily in order to identify and prepare qualified future employees. And there's a lot of truth to this: A 2007 survey of business coalitions found that workforce preparedness was their top motivation for getting involved in schooling (below).

But it would be a mistake to stop there: There are many reasons that business partners work with schools, and partners can have different priorities that change over time.

The key is to ask them what's important to them — what problems they're trying to solve by working with you. And remember to revisit that question with them from time to time, to make sure your partnership is continuing to meet their needs.

ROI: Customers

Businesses have always wanted to look good in their customers' eyes, and have found that working with nonprofits and other social institutions (like schools) is a great way to do that. The cause marketing industry calls it "doing well by doing good." By working with schools or nonprofit groups, businesses can see several benefits in the area of customer relations, including:

Survey of Business Leaders: What Types of Partnership Outcomes Are Most Important?

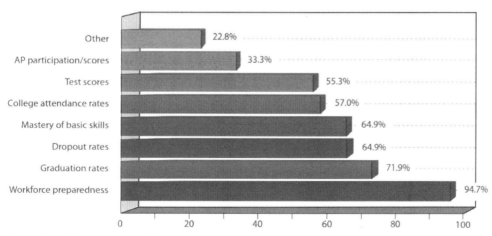

Source: DeHavilland Associates, 2007

◊ **Attracting new customers**: Most Americans will switch from one brand to another, assuming that price and quality are approximately the same, if the other brand is associated with a cause. And for new and old customers alike, more than half have indicated that corporate citizenship has some level of influence on their purchasing decisions.

◊ **Premium pricing**: Both consumers and business decision-makers are seven times more likely to pay a premium price for products and services to a company with a strong social reputation versus one with a poor reputation.

◊ **Brand strength**: Multiple studies show that consumers hold higher regard for companies and brands that demonstrate a commitment to working on social issues.

◊ **Positive word of mouth**: Nearly three-quarters of Americans say that a company's commitment to a social issue is a factor when deciding whether to recommend a company to others.

◊ **Influencing the influencers**: Evidence indicates that a company's commitment to a social issue influences the opinions of experts (including financial analysts, academics, and industry leaders) and reporting by the media.

To be clear, we're not talking about allowing your partners to market to your students and parents: This is not about distributing coupons or putting flyers

The Birth of Cause Marketing: The Campaign to Restore the Statue of Liberty

Businesses have been involved in their communities for decades, even centuries; but in 1983, just over 25 years ago, something happened to fundamentally change the way businesses think about their approach to community engagement. This change has since filtered through to other sectors that provide funds and resources to social causes.

In 1983, a civic group in New York City launched a campaign to clean up the Statue of Liberty, which had fallen into some disrepair. They approached several companies for financial support; one of these was American Express, from whom they requested a $1 million donation. The CEO at the time blanched at the number but made a counteroffer: American Express would promote the campaign to their cardmembers and the public, and would give the State of Liberty campaign 1 cent for every card transaction, and $1 for every new approved card application over a three-month period.

The public responded to the campaign, and American Express generated close to $1.7 million for the project. But they also realized some significant benefits for themselves. They found that, during the life of the campaign, transactions increased 28 percent, and new card applications rose by 45 percent — increases unmatched by any other marketing campaign from the company. Just as importantly, they saw that the company's brand image had

been strengthened, trade relations were significantly better, and employee morale had improved. In short, American Express found that by supporting a social venture, they were able to achieve business objectives — and the idea of cause marketing, and the broader concept of strategic philanthropy, was born.

Despite the fact that the first instance of strategic philanthropy occurred just over 25 years ago, the concept took hold in the business community and is now widespread, from Fortune 500 companies to locally owned businesses. They realize that their community engagement efforts can generate benefits to their organizations, and that they can make partnership decisions according to the promised return on their investment just as they do with marketing, operations, and other core functions.

There is clearly some awareness of this concept among nonprofits and others as well, given their increased focus on recognizing supporters through logo placements, ads, naming rights, and other types of recognition. But in reality, as American Express and many other companies have discovered, returns on a social investment can help accomplish an array of business objectives, and nonprofit and social organizations that understand that and can work with their partners to meet these objectives can attract a tremendous amount of support for their work.

into backpacks. What we are talking about is allowing your partners to look good as a result of the good work they're doing with you. If they're interested in customer relations, they may be interested in broadcasting their involvement in your programs by publicizing the partnership on in-store displays, using your school's logo on their website, including information about your partnership in their customer mailings, and more.

ROI: Human Resources

As every CTE teacher knows, business and education leaders understand the importance of developing the workforce of tomorrow, and that this serves as a primary motivation for companies to get involved in career exploration and preparedness programs. But companies that work with schools and nonprofits can also see immediate benefits when their existing workforce gets involved.

Surveys of employers and employees alike find that a company's work in the community increases employee morale, strengthens loyalty, and reduces employee turnover, and that campaigns that provide employees an opportunity to play an active role (such as volunteering) have a greater impact in those areas. A company's social reputation is also a factor in attracting future employees, making it easier to recruit talented staff and reducing associated recruiting costs.

Some companies also look at their partnerships with nonprofits as an opportunity to develop the skills and leadership qualities of their staff members. Deloitte Consulting, for example, has loaned out staff members on a full-time basis to take on major projects for partner organizations, which gives Deloitte employees an opportunity to develop their personal and professional skills while benefiting their partners; education organizations such as the National Academy Foundation have also benefited in the past from corporate talent on loan to them. Surveys of corporate managers confirm that these types of arrangements have helped employees to build skills and advance professionally.

ROI: Operations

While customers and employees are important stakeholders, companies have other stakeholders to consider as well, including investors, vendors, unions, and government regulators. A company's social commitment can influence these relationships as well. As an example, investors benefit when a company pursues a social agenda, with many studies showing a positive relationship between social and financial performance. And in terms of a company's "license to operate," the Conference Board has found clear evidence showing that poor corporate citizenship tends to invite regulatory or legal sanctions that lead to poor financial performance.

Operational considerations have particularly influenced the work of companies in regulated industries like cable television, financial services firms, and utilities. Campaigns designed for the classroom also show regulators how a company is contributing to its community, which helps to improve regulator relations and reduce the call for additional regulation in the future.

ROI: Individual Outcomes

So far, we've looked at how companies benefit from working with schools. But the individual businesspeople who work in these programs, sitting on advisory boards or mentoring students, see powerful benefits as well, including:

◊ **Intrinsic Rewards**: Companies look at the benefits of mentoring and volunteering in terms of employee morale and retention; for the people who do it, however, it's simpler to say that working with students makes us happier and more fulfilled and gives us a sense of purpose.

◊ **Affinity**: People want to belong. It may be that your volunteers feel an affinity with educators in their own families and want to work with students out of that motivation, or it may be that they feel an affinity with their company or the service group that has committed to your school. Regardless, they'll get personal rewards by working on behalf of their social group.

◊ **Resume Building/Skills Development**: If you give business partners leadership roles, like serving on your advisory board or heading up a committee, they'll be able to point to that experience and their accomplishments as part of their professional portfolio. The experience may also help them develop new skills that they'll be able to apply to their current or future jobs.

◊ **Networking**: Many partnership initiatives, like your advisory board or a career fair, bring businesspeople together from many different companies. These can serve as networking opportunities for your volunteers that can help them increase their connections to their industry or to the business community overall.

Incorporating ROI into Project Planning

Clearly there are a lot of benefits for companies and individuals who work with schools. Partnership leaders who highlight these kinds of benefits when talking with partners and, more importantly, are willing to design programs that line up with these goals, will have a tremendous advantage when soliciting support.

But remember this: While this list of possible benefits is helpful in giving you a sense of what companies might be interested in, every partner is unique. You can't just assume that you know what's going to be important to your partners. In every case, you need to sit down with them and ask: What's important to your company? What challenges do you have? What are you trying to accomplish?

The only way to find out what return they're interested in is to ask. But once you invest the time to find out (and very few actually do), you'll be in a very strong position to build a partnership that benefits everyone at the table.

1.6 How Educators Benefit from Partnerships

As we think about how to engage the business community in education, it makes sense to look at the benefits they can get from their investment. But it's just as important to look at the benefits to schools and educators: For a partnership to work, every partner has to see the advantages of contributing their time and resources to the effort.

It's easy to skip over the benefits to educators by simply saying "they're in it for the kids." Of course they're interested in student outcomes; and, as noted elsewhere, there are lots of ways that partnerships can help students. But there are lots of ways to help students that don't involve all the work of partnership development; because of the lack of a compelling ROI, partnerships have remained as a "nice to have" item rather than a "have to have."

To make partnerships worthwhile, we have to look specifically at how partnerships can benefit teachers and their schools.

Partnerships: Good for Schools and Educators

Of course, schools and teachers "win" when they see improved student outcomes as outlined above, not only for the sake of the students, but also because the schools are judged on outcomes such as graduation rates and proficiency scores. But they also see direct benefits from working with business partners, such as:

◊ **Better Market Information**. Schools, and CTE programs in particular, can only truly succeed if the education they provide to their students lines up with the realities students will face once they leave school. But for some CTE teachers, it has been a number of years since they directly participated in the workforce. Technology, procedures, and standards have changed significantly, yet their first-hand perspective is locked in previous decades. Strong business involvement keeps them current.

◊ **Improved Access to Resources**. In a time of flat or declining budgets, the support that partners provide can make a huge impact on school operations and student services. This includes not only financial support, but gifts of time (volunteers) and goods and services.

◊ **Improved Employee Morale**. Teachers and administrators who are connected to the community through partnerships feel more confident and better-supported in their work; when they become involved in industry work through training and externships, their morale and confidence (not to mention knowledge and skills) improves further.

◊ **Better Staff Support and Development**. There are many partnerships in which teachers receive externship and training opportunities, allowing them to stay connected to the industry and keep up with current information and practices. Partnerships can also help teachers become more comfortable with new content areas or give them new ways to engage students with existing content. Administrators can benefit as well: There are several partnerships in which CEOs have served as executive mentors to new principals, helping them learn to manage time, facilities, change, and culture.

◊ **Understanding**: In many communities, there is a real disconnect between schools and the business community; part of this comes from the fact that, unless they have firsthand experience with their schools, businesspeople may not understand the challenges that schools are facing, ranging from big challenges like poverty issues to smaller ones like paperwork requirements and approval processes. Partnerships are a way to bring businesspeople into the schools to let them see what's happening firsthand and serve as ambassadors to the community.

◊ **Opportunities for Students**: Most educators, particularly those in CTE, have seen time after time how much of an impact real-world experiences can have on students. They learn how businesses work; they learn how to conduct themselves professionally; they see the relevance of what they're learning in the classroom; they become more engaged; and they have a much clearer sense of direction. Working with business partners makes all of these opportunities possible.

As you work with your business partners to develop your partnership plans, remember to spend just as much time focusing on the education ROI as you do on the business ROI: It's just as important to keep your teachers engaged and your administrators on board as it is to gain buy-in from your businesses.

1.7 What Businesses Bring to the Table

Determining which resources are available to fuel your partnership work should be one of your first considerations; but too often, this conversation tends to happen closer to the end of the process. Partners can be so focused on building a program that they don't consider the role of resources in the equation.

Unfortunately, this oversight can limit the size and strength of your partnership. If you don't know what your partners can provide, you could end up with a small pool of resources to fuel your campaign. You may end up with a mismatch, such as pushing for a mentoring program with a partner who has few employees interested in the commitment, when that same partner has valuable equipment sitting in storage that could have been donated had anyone asked.

When business partners have a role in the selection of outcomes and the design of the partnership program, not only will they be more committed to the project as co-owners, but you'll also be able to create the program in a way that takes advantage of all the resources your partners can make available to you.

Opening the Door to the Asset Discussion

As you work through the development process with your prospective partners, assets should never be the first item on the agenda: It is important to first find common ground in terms of desired student outcomes, along with a realization that all partners must receive some benefits from the relationship. You should take the time to find out what benefits are important to each individual partner: You may know generally how businesses can benefit from these sorts of initiatives, but you cannot make headway until you understand what kinds of outcomes your individual partners want to achieve.

This line of inquiry is important for two reasons: First, it allows you to structure a program that can meet the needs of your partner, creating a return on their investment that will keep them committed over the long haul. And second, paying attention to the results they want to achieve creates an atmosphere of trust that is critical when asking about the resources they might want to contribute to the partnership.

Going Beyond Money

Financial support is always welcome, of course, but experienced partnership leaders intentionally stay away from asking for funds during the early stages of a relationship. Financial gifts limit engagement and commitment, and if you fail to build a strong foundation for the partnership, you'll end up seeing limited interest and support on the part of your partners.

In reality, partners can provide support in a wide range of ways. As you explore what resources might be available for your partnership, look at the following:

Employee time

Look at the number of employees at local partner sites as well as their skills, time availability, and level of interest. You may find a volunteer force for classroom activities or improvement projects; mentors to work with students on professional or personal development; or even highly skilled specialists who can act as consultants to handle more challenging tasks, such as researchers who can support curriculum selection efforts, managers of large facilities who can help look for efficiencies in your current maintenance procedures, or PR professionals who can assist with the development of your website or community outreach materials.

Donated goods and services

Consider how some businesses structure their contributions to causes they consider to be worthy. When asked for support, airlines are sometimes willing to donate free tickets, which can help nonprofits defray costs or be raffled off as fundraisers, while restaurants may provide food for volunteers or vouchers, which again can be used in raffles or giveaways. Some goods or services, such as landscaping or cable service, can be provided at no cost to your school or district to help with operations or instruction.

In each case, these organizations are leveraging the assets they have in greatest supply and that cost them the least to provide. You should pursue this line of thinking by looking for the assets your current and prospective partners can most easily contribute and consider how they can tie in to your work.

An Innovative Use of Assets: The Simon Youth Foundation

It almost sounds like something you'd hear from a stand-up comedian — "if kids are skipping school and hanging out at the mall, why not put a school there?" But for Simon Property Group, which manages some of the most prominent mall properties in America, it was a serious idea that made imminent sense — and over the years they've changed thousands of lives by acting on it.

After seeing the impact of a couple of local programs on reaching youth through mall-driven initiatives, executives at Simon Property Group came together to see how they could develop a coordinated, national approach. After reviewing the resources available to them, they developed a strategy to leverage unused mall space to house satellite public schools and to then provide those schools with enhanced support. The Simon Youth Foundation (SYF) was created to launch and manage this initiative, which now features 23 Simon Youth Academies in 13 states. SYF has maintained a 90 percent graduation rate at its Academies since inception, graduated more than 10,000 students, and awarded more than $10 million in scholarships.

It starts with a commitment to make mall space available to local schools interested in setting up a small satellite school to serve students at risk of dropping out. Simon Youth Foundation makes the space available for free to its partner districts, and commits to spending between $250,000 and $350,000 to build out the space to make it an appropriate learning environment. Beyond that, SYF also agrees to refresh each site on a five-year schedule (new paint, carpet, etc.), or possibly more often if a visual inspection indicates that there is a need.

School districts are responsible for paying utility expenses, which are generally available at a lower rate given the volume discounts available to large sites such as malls. District partners are also responsible for any equipment needed at the school, such as desks and computers, though SYF does look for opportunities to contribute resources in those areas when feasible.

Each Academy is staffed completely by the district, including administrators, teachers, counselors and other support personnel. While SYF does not cover the costs of personnel, it does support staff with professional development opportunities, including hosting them at an annual meeting, where teachers and administrators can share thoughts and ideas, and receive training on working with target populations. SYF also offers each site an "enhancement grant," which provides them the extra funding they need for discretionary purchases such as field trips, extra curricular materials, recognition ceremonies and rewards for achieving students, and other types of initiatives not covered through regular funding channels.

Other product/service donations

Look beyond the products or services your partner provides and consider what goes into their production in order to find potential hidden assets. If they manufacture products, do they have used equipment they could donate, or would they invite your CTE instructors to existing on-site trainings in the latest techniques? Can service providers help you find better pricing on materials you both buy? Can they train your staff in their areas of expertise? Do these partners have unused office space you can use in some way?

Expertise and strengths

Consider what strengths your partner company may have. These may be what your partner is known for, or they may be hidden strengths that nevertheless could provide great value to your work. For example, newspaper companies are known for their journalistic and publishing capabilities, but a lesser-known strength is their expertise in logistics — getting thousands of newspapers to readers and retailers each day. Along these lines, consider whether they have a strong brand, a proven distribution network, or some other capabilities that could be called on.

Relationships

Partners may have relationships with others that could support your work. Do they belong to the local chamber, and can they introduce you to additional partners? Do they belong to industry associations or have access to industry experts that could guide your work? Do they have agreements with celebrity spokespeople?

Outreach

Whether your partners market to consumers or to businesspeople, they have access to marketing channels that may benefit your work. If your partner sends bills to customers, there may be an opportunity to add a bill stuffer; if they advertise in trade publications, perhaps they could highlight your partnership (and Web address!) in their ads.

The key when holding a discussion about available assets is to assure your partner that you're not trying to squeeze every resource out of them: you're simply trying to design a program that can have as much impact as possible, which means working with the resources that are easiest for partners to contribute.

And one final note: If your contact represents just one department within a larger organization, find out whether other departments may have an interest in your work. If your initiative appeals to your community relations contact as well as their HR representative, you may be able to tap into an entirely new source of resources within the same partner organization.

Partnership Planning Worksheet: Asset Analysis, Business Partners

You can either share this worksheet with your business partners or you can use it as a checklist to make sure that neither of you overlook any opportunities that would be attractive to them.

What do we already offer to schools?
(ex: grants, volunteers, internships)

What do we produce or offer? What about the tools/resources used? *(ex: donating products or services, providing access to tools or equipment)*

What other physical assets could we access?
(ex: excess space, vans or buses)

What strengths do we have? What are we known for? *(ex: logistics, market knowledge)*

What kinds of skill sets do our local employees have, and how could those be applied? *(ex: technical skills, management skills, marketing)*

How do we currently train our people? Could that training be shared with students or teachers?

What relationships do we have that may be valuable? *(ex: industry contacts, vendors)*

What other departments in the company might get involved? *(ex: human resources, community relations)*

1.8 What Schools Bring to the Table

One of the essential principles of good partnerships is that partners come to the table as equals, each making an investment in the partnership, and each getting some kind of benefit in return for that investment. For some reason, educators often shortchange the value that they bring to the table; they see the value in the things that their partners contribute, but fail to see the value in their own contributions.

It's important for schools to not only realize the value they bring to the partnership, but also make sure that their partners clearly understand that value. When business coalition leaders were asked in a 2007 survey, "What criteria do you use when selecting partners," 64 percent said it was important that their education partners had made a commitment to the project, meaning some kind of real investment. And in most cases, educators are making those investments; they just need to recognize it and share the information with their partners.

Schools invest in their partnerships in a number of ways:

◊ **Staff** – Most partnerships involve staff time, whether it's the time of teachers, counselors, or administrators (and sometimes all three). These people may be working on the clock, in which case their time is a financial investment being made by the school, or they may be working on their own, in which case they are making a personal investment. In either case, their time has value and this should be recognized.

◊ **Facilities** – If partnership events happen on school grounds, such as in the classroom, the auditorium, or the gym, there is a value associated with that space, just as if you had to rent space elsewhere to host such events. This includes not only the space itself but also services such as security and janitorial services.

◊ **Inclusion in the curriculum** – Surprisingly, a great number of business partnerships happen outside of school, either after-hours and/or off-site. Finding meaningful ways of including partnership activities within the curriculum, such as attaching a grade to a team-based partnership project or allowing class time for mentoring activities, adds value to the initiative in the eyes of your partner.

◊ **Expertise** – Most businesspeople recognize that they don't have a background in instruction or curriculum design; your school, district, or state-level staff can add value to a project by sharing their instructional expertise to the design and implementation of a project.

◊ **Transportation** – If a partnership requires sponsored transportation, such as taking students on a local site visit or across the state for a competition, schools often provide vehicles and cover the costs of a driver and fuel.

◊ **Paperwork** – In many partnerships, some level of paperwork is required, a responsibility usually assumed by the school partners. One example would be background checks, which most schools require before adults have direct contact with students; another example would be a written application for use of school facilities.

◊ **Parent outreach** – Schools have a direct pipeline to parents, and can solicit support for programs, particularly those that take place off-site or after school and require extra commitment from parents in the form of costs or transportation requirements. Schools can also handle administrative details like distributing and collecting permission slips and liability waivers.

◊ **Access to other partners** – It's likely that the business partner you're currently talking to isn't your only partner; in fact, you may have other relationships, perhaps with postsecondary institutions or nonprofit organizations (ex: mentoring associations, community service groups) who could be valuable additions to the partnership ideas you're discussing, allowing you to play a "connector" role.

◊ **Access to data** – It's very difficult for external partners to get good data on student outcomes through partnership initiatives; your school or district may be able to access data that allows you and your partners to better track the progress of student participants (while honoring all confidentiality policies and laws of course).

◊ **Partner benefits** – Many schools recognize their business partners with banners and mentions in their e-newsletters; this is valuable for your partners, as is the ability to connect them at a professional level with your other partners. Businesspeople who sit on advisory boards, for example, benefit greatly from the networking opportunities that board meetings provide.

There may be other contributions that schools can make to partnerships, but these constitute some of the more common ones; consider these and others as you catalog the ways in which you're supporting your partnership efforts.

Partnership Planning Worksheet: Asset Analysis, Education Partners

You can work through this worksheet prior to meeting with your business partners (so you have a clear sense of what you bring to the table) or you can work through it together as part of a collaborative process.

Can educators be involved in partnerships during school hours? Can we enable them to be involved outside school hours?

Can our facilities be used for partnership events? Can that include non-classroom locations for special events?

Where appropriate, can we include partnership activities in the classroom? Can they count towards grades or class credit?

Can we access school or district transportation resources for activities during or after school?

Can we manage required paperwork, such as handling background checks, getting district approval for projects as needed, and getting permission slips signed?

Do we have other partners who may provide value to new partnerships? *(ex: postsecondary partners, mentoring organizations)*

Can we provide access to data so that partnership efforts are tracked and assessed?

What can we provide that will directly benefit our partners? *(ex: recognition, networking opportunities)*

1.9 The Partnership Pyramid

People tend to talk about partnerships as a single, "catch-all" category, when in reality the level of support schools receive from different partners can vary quite a bit. We call local citizens our partners when they vote for school bonds, and use the same term when referring to the local business that contributes thousands of dollars and volunteer hours. While any support is appreciated, of course, using a single term can cloud our thinking on the subject; it can also limit what people may contribute when we ask them to partner with us.

When asking the question, "What does it mean to be a partner?" understand that there are different levels of partnering. Defining these levels may help in targeting partnership opportunities and in talking with members of your community about how they can contribute to K–12 education in your area.

Level I: Foundational Community Support

At the most fundamental level, everyone in a school's service area is a stakeholder, whether they are a parent, community leader, or taxpayer. Their

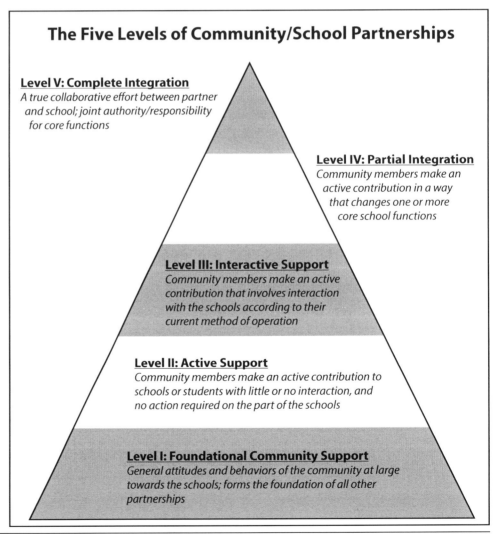

The Five Levels of Community/School Partnerships

Level V: Complete Integration
A true collaborative effort between partner and school; joint authority/responsibility for core functions

Level IV: Partial Integration
Community members make an active contribution in a way that changes one or more core school functions

Level III: Interactive Support
Community members make an active contribution that involves interaction with the schools according to their current method of operation

Level II: Active Support
Community members make an active contribution to schools or students with little or no interaction, and no action required on the part of the schools

Level I: Foundational Community Support
General attitudes and behaviors of the community at large towards the schools; forms the foundation of all other partnerships

positive attitudes on, and behaviors toward, area schools can be considered as a basic type of support.

Examples of partners at this level would include community members who hold favorable attitudes toward local schools; decide to enroll their children in those schools; vote for school bond issuances; and speak favorably about the schools or district, both privately and publicly.

A supportive community is an essential foundation for the other, more active types of partnerships found higher on the pyramid at right. If there is little or no goodwill among the community, it will be much more difficult to establish a broad base of active partnerships with individual stakeholders or groups.

Self-Assessment:

What is your current level of community support?

_____ *What percentage of school-aged children in your community go to public schools?*

_____ *What percentage of recent bond proposals have passed?*

_____ *Is the business community supportive or critical of the schools?*

_____ *What is the general tone of community discussion regarding area schools?*

You'll probably not be able to make a big dent in these factors (at least not right away), but it's helpful to understand the environment you're working in.

Level II: Active Support

The next level up consists of active support from community members and individual stakeholders or groups. At this level, people make an active contribution to their area schools, but they have little or no contact with students, teachers, or administrators, and their work does not change the existing operations of the school in material ways.

There are many examples of this type of support:

◊ Individuals or businesses donating to support an extracurricular function, such as underwriting the cost of band uniforms or athletic equipment

◊ Members of a civic organization, or groups of employees, volunteering to clean up the school grounds on a designated volunteer day

◊ A local food bank managing a weekend backpack program for students in high-poverty areas

- ◊ Businesses donating used equipment to a CTE program

- ◊ Individuals or businesses donating prizes for raffles or student contests

- ◊ A local restaurant offering free food for an event or an off-site meeting room

In each of these examples, there is little or no direct interaction with students or staff, and the partnerships do not affect standard school operations. But that doesn't mean that these types of partnerships are not important: They either improve the quality or richness of students' educational experience or allow the district to forego expenses they might otherwise incur.

Exercise:

List three partners working at the Active level.

_____

_____

_____

Can these partners be moved up the pyramid in some way?

Level III: Interactive Support

At the third level, stakeholder partnerships are active and interactive activities. They place partners in direct contact with students and staff and often tie directly to academic or other measured outcomes such as postsecondary planning or dropout prevention.

Examples of Level III partnerships include:

- ◊ Members of a local chamber hosting a career day or visiting classes to talk about their industries

- ◊ A local business establishes a mentoring program or student internship initiative

- ◊ A business/education coalition creates a summer externship program for teachers, exposing them to current practices in their field

- ◊ A civic organization commits to a regular reading program with a specific classroom

- ◊ An organization adopts a school and helps the administration meet identified needs

Partners at this level are working to help students and schools achieve goals that are already in place, and their efforts are supplemental to the core learning experience. While such partnerships can produce significant benefits for students, they do not change the way schools operate academically or operationally.

Exercise:

List three partners working at the Interactive level.

_____

_____

_____

Can these partners be moved up the pyramid in some way?

Level IV: Partial Integration

At the next level, partners take on a more equal role with their school, acting as much like a collaborator as a supporter. This entails a greater commitment and level of responsibility on the part of the community partner.

Individual examples of these kinds of partnerships include:

◊ A committee of high-level business executives working with the Montgomery County Business Roundtable for Education partnered with the Montgomery County (Maryland) Public Schools to analyze current district operations in targeted areas and recommend efficiencies, ultimately saving the district hundreds of thousands of dollars each year

◊ Simon Property Group, a property manager overseeing malls across the country, works with 24 districts in 12 states to host alternative learning school sites within their properties at no cost to their partner districts

◊ The Gowan Company worked with the Crane School District in Yuma, Arizona, to build a science/math program for advanced students, paying for teacher salaries, technology, curriculum, and supplemental resources

In each of these examples, the school district was open to changing some element of its operation, whether it involved a new school site, existing district operations, or creation of a new academic strand, and worked with their partner as a collaborator to make that happen. In each case, this resulted in dramatic and positive results for the participating district.

Exercise:

List three partners working at the Partial Integration level.

_____

_____

_____

Can these partners be moved up the pyramid in some way?

Level V: Complete Integration

Complete Integration includes situations where schools and their stakeholders become true partners, working together to define the purpose of education, collaboratively determining how to achieve those goals, and sharing the responsibility and authority to make it all happen. One of the few examples available would be the academies of the National Academy Foundation, which use customized, career-specific curricula and rely on local businesspeople for significant portions of the learning process. Organizations that launch charter schools would be another example.

Exercise:

List two partners working at the Complete Integration level.

_____

_____

Can these partnerships be replicated at other sites or with other partners? Can you use these partnerships to showcase your work with other stakeholders?

The opportunity here is to identify the relationships that exist at each level and try to move them up the ladder. Look at your Active partnerships and look for ways to make them Interactive. But understand that the pyramid model requires a strong base at each level to support the levels above them: You'll have more Interactive partnerships than Partial Integration partnerships. The increased commitment at each level means that you'll have fewer available partners able to make that commitment.

It is important to remember that all partnerships are important, no matter the size or scope. But hopefully by identifying the different types of partnerships and talking with partners and colleagues in these terms, we can think about new ways to engage stakeholders and fully utilize their contributions for the benefit of our students.

Partnership Planning Worksheet: The Partnership Pyramid

Look through the definitions throughout this section and list some of your partners at each level of the partnership pyramid. Once you've identified specific companies, think about how you can move them up the pyramid.

Level V: Complete Integration
1. _____
2. _____
3. _____

Level IV: Partial Integration
1. _____
2. _____
3. _____

Level III: Interactive Support
1. _____
2. _____
3. _____

Level II: Active Support
1. _____
2. _____
3. _____

Level I: Foundational Community Support
1. _____
2. _____
3. _____

How to Work with Partners

2.1 Advisory Boards

> **NOTE**: *The Employer Engagement Toolkit devotes an entire section to advisory boards (Section VI, "Deep Dive: Advisory Boards"). This unit offers basic information on the purpose and basic elements of advisory boards; see Section VI for in-depth coverage.*

It is extremely difficult to build a strong and effective CTE program without having a strong and effective advisory board. The advisory board serves as a gateway to the business community, providing an easy way for business leaders to learn more about your work and how it relates to their needs, just as it serves as a way for you to learn more about their needs so you can better prepare your students. In short, it provides the community with a window into your program, and provides your program with a window into the community.

Most states require that CTE programs have an advisory board and mandate a minimum number of members and a minimum number of meetings per year. It's important to realize that these are, in fact, minimum expectations: You'll get out of your advisory board what you put into it, and you'll need to go well beyond state-mandated minimums if you want to reap the rewards that an effective board can offer.

Benefits of an Advisory Board

What benefits can a strong advisory board offer to your program? There are several, including:

◊　**Real-time industry information that helps you set the right outcomes for your programs.** CTE programs exist in order to prepare students for real-world opportunities. But if you don't have current information on industry requirements and expectations — if you don't know what types of positions employers are hiring for, and if you don't know what they expect of their employees — it will be extremely difficult to adequately prepare your students. Your board can play a critically important role in keeping your program aligned with the industry it serves.

◊　**An increase in community support, including more volunteers and more resources.** You'll of course have business partners outside of your advisory board; but your board, which will include representatives from some of the largest employers in your field, will have the best information about your needs and the greatest ability to meet those needs.

◊　**Increased access to student and staff development opportunities.** Work-based learning is a core element of any CTE program, and your advisory board members will be well-positioned to respond to the needs of your program, both through their own companies and through their network of connections. Work-based learning opportunities include openings for students, including site visits, job shadowing opportunities, and internships, as well as opportunities for educators such as summer externships to keep them connected to their profession and to others in their field.

◊ **Stronger community awareness and support, particularly within the business community.** In addition to being influential representatives of your industry in their own right, your board members can connect you with dozens or even hundreds of others in the business community. Committed board members are excellent ambassadors and advocates for your program, spreading the word about your work and inviting others to join in as volunteers and supporters.

Board Structure

There is no one correct way to structure an advisory board. Many schools simply have a single board for each of their CTE programs, with each board meeting and working together as a group. Others may have multiple boards, including an executive board at the district level (particularly when multiple schools offer the same programs) reinforced with school-level boards; furthermore, those boards may have multiple committees charged with addressing specific issues on behalf of the board (such as workforce alignment, work-based learning, fundraising, or building postsecondary relationships).

If you're just starting out, keep things as simple as possible: Find a handful of committed partners to serve as your inaugural advisory board, build out your board as needed (with leadership and support from this initial group of board members), and then consider committees when an issue requires a special focus outside of general board functions.

Makeup of Your Board

As a general rule, you'll want 75 percent of your board members to come from the business community, with the total number of members depending on the size of your industry's presence within your community. Business representatives should include the following:

◊ Representatives from some of the largest, more established employers in industries relevant to your programs; these will be the companies that employ the largest number of your graduates.

◊ Representatives from some of the smaller but fast-growing companies in industries relevant to your program.

◊ A senior executive with extensive management experience, particularly to fill the oversight role

◊ A leader from a connector organization such as your local chamber of commerce, workforce investment board, or economic development council, who can give you a broad perspective on your industry and related industries and also connect you with companies in your field for market information and student and teacher opportunities.

◊ A leader from any local professional or trade associations who will be active in promoting the growth of your field and attuned to the education and training needs of your profession.

In addition to these industry representatives (which make up 75 percent of your board), you'll want to round out your board with some of the following types of people:

◊ Professionals from related postsecondary programs in the area

◊ Past students, or parents of current/former students

◊ One or two teachers, though there is no consensus on this. Some program leaders include educators on their boards to provide a classroom perspective; others exclude teachers out of a concern that business representatives may be less comfortable sharing their concerns or critiques in their presence.

Common Advisory Board Activities

Your board activities will vary widely on the basis of your board's scope of authority and the timing of any major initiatives. But here are a few of the areas in which boards are commonly involved on an ongoing basis:

◊ **Program Alignment** – This is one of the core functions of your board, and should be addressed throughout the year. This includes discussing current and future workforce requirements and how your program responds to those needs in terms of curriculum, sequence of courses, industry engagement, accreditation, and focus on certifications.

◊ **Community Engagement** – Your partners are an important source of connections to your industry, and should regularly discuss attracting new partners and exploring new work-based learning opportunities for students and staff.

◊ **Major Initiatives** – As your board engages in major projects, such as capital campaigns or advocacy, you'll want your board to keep regular tabs on progress.

◊ **Collaborative Discussions** – Your board should regularly raise and address concerns and big-picture issues related to your program. Your board members are there because you wanted access to their expertise: Take advantage of that.

Remember, there is no one right way to structure a board, and there is no one right way to run one: Focus on building a board that addresses the unique circumstances and needs of your program and your industry.

2.2 Expertise

Because CTE is so focused on producing real-world, professional-level outcomes, educators in this field are experienced in spotting talent and connecting it to their programs. Teachers are generally very good at enhancing instruction by connecting students to professionals in various ways, from guest speaking roles to internships.

Usually, however, this happens just at the program level and consists of plugging people into the existing instructional plan. What would happen if you were to fully harness the skills and expertise of your partners, shaping instruction to take advantage of all that they can offer? Better yet, what would happen if you connected their expertise to your school-wide vision?

For example:

◊ The architect who talks to students about his job could be helping you design an extension to your building or envision a design lab.

◊ The marketing pro who mentors one of your business students could help you develop a campaign to recruit rising ninth graders, or help you redesign your website.

◊ The HVAC company owner who takes students as interns could help you do an energy audit and create a plan to improve energy efficiency (and lower costs!) in your building.

This is commonly referred to as "skills-based volunteering," and this is actually the area in which business partners most want to contribute (see chart below).

Types of Support from Business Partners
On a scale of 1–5, with 1 being "no support" and 5 being "a major category of support," rank the following by the level of support you provide directly to your school/district partners:

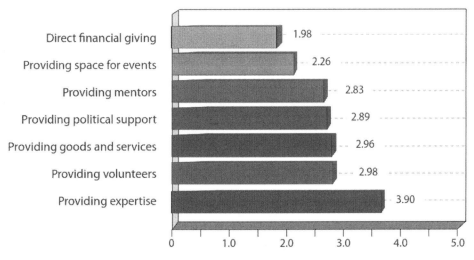

Source: Coalition Leaders Speak Out on Education, DeHavilland Associates, 2007

There are a few areas in particular that can benefit from this kind of support:

Instruction

CTE teachers are already very good at connecting with professionals and plugging them into their existing lesson plans. They should consider recruiting experts who can help them revise their curricula to reflect modern standards or different teaching strategies, and who can help create new opportunities for students, such as competitions these experts can judge, or projects that these experts can structure and guide. As an example, some construction programs take on building projects that rely on the expertise of local builders, electricians, and others who work with students as they design and implement the project.

Advisory Boards

We invite industry members to sit on our advisory boards in part on the basis of their expertise in their professional areas. But how many advisory boards are tapping into the talents of existing members, or recruiting new members with skills needed in key areas? If your program is facing financial challenges, do you have someone with financial or fundraising expertise on the board, and have they been asked for guidance? If you're interested in improving your use of data, do you have an IT expert on hand?

Management/Operations

When we talk about experts, our thoughts usually go immediately to how they can support instruction. But if your experts can improve operations, staff and students alike will have a better learning environment, and you may be able to free up funds through improved operations that can then be directed into instruction. That was the case with Montgomery County (Maryland) Public Schools, where members of the local business/education partnership group served as consultants on district operations and helped the district save hundreds of thousands of dollars a year, which were redirected into instruction. (See the "Operation Excellence" case study in Section VII for more on this example.)

Special Projects

Experts can also be recruited for one-time projects, without the ongoing commitment of an advisory board relationship. For example, College Summit (a nonprofit that connects low-income youth to college and career opportunities), which relies on real-time student performance data, had an IT system that didn't work to the standards they needed. Deloitte Consulting offered them a team of IT experts for six months to redesign and rebuild their IT system, saving them millions and making their work possible.

Exercise #1

If you're interested in leveraging the expertise of your partners, start by thinking big: Namely, asking your advisory board to help you build a vision for what your program or school could be within the next three to five years and what it would take to get there. Ask your teachers to come up with a similar vision for their programs: If they could do anything they wanted in order to teach their kids, what would they do?

These goals can be a combination of your ongoing annual planning and a "stretch list," things you'd like to accomplish but would be hard-pressed to make happen under current constraints.

List your major goals; for each, list the critical steps that would have to take place. Then, next to each of those critical steps, think about the individuals or companies in your network who have the skill sets to make those steps happen. Finally, think about how that project could be packaged as a limited-term, high-value partnership.

Example:

GOAL	CRITICAL STEPS	SKILLS-BASED VOLUNTEER
Build a green energy annex	*Raise $2 million*	*Fundraising expert/grant writer*
Design facility		*Architect/green energy expert*
Build facility		*Contractor*

With that list in hand, it's time to start networking: Start with your advisory board members and current volunteers, and network out from that circle of close connections to see if you can find experts interested in showcasing themselves by working with you. It may be hard to find expert volunteers in every area, but if even some of these can be provided pro bono, your dreams can become possible very quickly. And there are clear benefits to your partners: aside from the personal rewards, the architect can use his design for you as a showcase, and the contractor can use the opportunity to develop relationships with future employees, both now and in the future.

Exercise #2

Starting with goals in mind is one approach; another is to find interested people with relevant skills, and work with them to build a vision of how you could work together. Start with those already in your circle, including advisory board members, current partners, volunteers, and even parents of the students in your classes. How well do you know these contacts? Have you learned about their skill sets, both current skills and those from previous roles? Do you have copies of their resumes or bios?

Start interviewing your contacts, either formally or informally, to learn more about their areas of experience and skills. Use the chart on the following page as an example:

CONTACT	SKILLS	HOW THEY CAN BE APPLIED
Bill Davis	*Manager*	• *Executive mentor* • *Project manager for major program*
	Sales executive	• *Recruit partners* • *Solicit major donors* • *Help craft our presentation* • *Design strategy to promote our next bond offering*

Remember that your business contacts may have skills and experiences in other areas of their lives as well, such as expertise or abilities developed through civic engagement or personal hobbies or interests.

Once you've done an inventory of existing partners' skill sets, try to work out from there to your next tier of contacts; ask teachers and administrators to consider the skills and strengths of their contacts, and then perhaps start talking with others in your network.

One Company's Take on Skills-Based Volunteering

Many larger businesses encourage employees to volunteer in the community, and schools in particular have benefited from these corporate volunteer programs: businesspeople are often found reading to or mentoring children, helping teachers, or improving facilities. But is this the greatest value these volunteers can bring?

Deloitte, one of the largest consulting firms in the country, began asking this question four years ago. The firm had a long-standing commitment to community involvement, which was fulfilled both through direct giving and through the volunteer efforts of its workforce. As it sought ways to increase the impact of its efforts, company officials began looking at the utilization of its volunteering employees.

According to Lori Grey, Senior Manager for Public Relations and Community Involvement at Deloitte, "When we looked at the value of our employees' time, we saw that their volunteer work was valued at around $18 an hour - but the value of their professional time was much higher. And so we wondered whether there were opportunities for our people to provide greater value by contributing their professional skills."

Through their own analysis, coupled with the results of annual internal surveys, Deloitte's community involvement

team determined that skills-based volunteering could provide a marked increase in value to the communities in which it works, while at the same time fulfilling internal objectives such as skills and leadership development.

In addition to promoting skills-based volunteering to employees and to the nonprofit community, Deloitte has taken steps to build awareness of the concept, including:

- Launching the Problem Solvers Fund, which provides grants to support community initiatives where Deloitte employees are engaged in pro bono and other skills-based volunteer projects.
- Supporting, and participating in, the Pro Bono Action Tank, an initiative of the Taproot Foundation to promote skills-based volunteering and public/private partnerships.
- Establishing a national partnership with College Summit, providing funding and expertise to help in areas such as improving the capabilities and speed of their data reporting system.

"Educating employees and nonprofits about the value of skills-based volunteering is an ongoing process," says Lori Grey, "but the benefits are substantial for everyone involved. This will continue to be an area of focus for us."

2.3 Mentors

Mentoring can be a very effective work-based learning activity in which your business partners and other community leaders can engage. Mentoring not only improves the lives of the students (known as mentees), but also has been shown to improve the personal and professional lives of the business leaders (mentors). Mentors can come from the advisory board, higher education, the business community, or from civic or religious organizations in your community.

The role of the mentor is to encourage, motivate, and support the success of the students in the program and to help the students achieve their goals in high school, in college, and in their careers. Just like a goal of 100 percent of students getting a paid internship, CTE program leaders should strive to provide 100 percent of students in the program with a mentor. Business leaders may be able to mentor more than one student until enough mentors can be recruited to provide a one-on-one mentor for every student, or they may mentor in teams.

Mentors can assist in many ways, including but not limited to:

◊ Making network business connections for the students

◊ Assisting with homework

◊ Assisting with college applications

◊ Assisting with financial aid applications

◊ Assisting with studying for SATs/ACTs

◊ Encouraging students to participate in high school and community events

◊ Assisting with career and life planning

◊ Assisting with personal financial planning

◊ Starting a journal

◊ Writing a book

◊ Going on a field trip

◊ Supervising peer-to-peer mentoring (ex: Seniors mentoring freshmen, juniors mentoring middle schoolers)

While many people see mentoring as a form of social support for young people (and it is powerful in this regard), it is also effective as a model for improving academic outcomes, helping students explore postsecondary and professional opportunities, and helping students make concrete plans for their futures.

Researching Other Ways for Mentors to Get Involved

There are dozens of websites and other resources to help you learn more about mentoring models, research showing the effectiveness of mentors, and ways for those in the business community to get involved in mentoring. Use the following list to learn more:

◊ www.mentoring.org

◊ www.juniorachievement.org/web/ja-usa/home

◊ http://educationnorthwest.org/resource/647

◊ www.coachingandmentoring.com/Mentor/contract.htm

◊ www.unl.edu/mentoring/MentoringWorksheet6.pdf

◊ www.nationalservice.gov/programs/americorps

◊ www.nationalservice.gov/pdf/06_0503_mentoring_factsheet.pdf

◊ www.ehow.com/list_6539947_high-school-mentoring-activities.html

◊ http://oemanagement.com/data/_files/mentoring.pdf

◊ www.ehow.com/info_8577678_schoolbased-mentoring-activities.html

◊ www.ehow.com/info_12017564_fun-group-mentoring-activities.html

◊ www.ehow.com/list_7644679_mentoring-checklist.html

Structure of Mentoring

Mentors should "meet" with their mentees regularly for 30–60 minutes. The frequency of these meetings may somewhat depend on the availability of the mentor but should occur no less frequently than monthly. These "meetings" most likely should take place face to face at the school where the environment is safe and controlled for both the student and the mentor. Meetings could also include meeting by e-mail or Skype or through a social network, but these interactions shouldn't substitute for face-to-face meetings. In some cases, particularly where mentors are pressed for time, you may arrange for transportation to have students meet with their Mentors at their places of business. (See the "Luxottica Mentoring Partnership" case study in Section VII for more.)

Appropriate care and protection for both the students and the mentors should be taken, including:

◊ Background checks

◊ Fingerprinting

◊ Copying the program director or school counselor on ALL emails

Elements of Effective Practice for Mentoring

Standard 1: Recruitment

Benchmarks:

Mentor Recruitment

B.1.1   Program engages in recruitment strategies that realistically portray the benefits, practices, and challenges of mentoring in the program.

Mentee Recruitment

B.1.2   Program recruits youth whose needs best match the services offered by the program and helps them understand what mentoring is and what they can expect from a mentoring relationship.

Enhancements:

Mentor Recruitment

E.1.1   Program has a written statement outlining eligibility requirements for mentors in its program.

Mentee Recruitment

E.1.2   Program has a written statement outlining eligibility requirements for mentees in its program.

Standard 2: Screening

Benchmarks:

Mentor Screening

B.2.1   Mentor completes an application.

B.2.2   Mentor agrees to a one (calendar or school) year minimum commitment for the mentoring relationship.

B.2.3   Mentor agrees to participate in face-to-face meetings with his or her mentee that average one time per week and one hour per meeting over the course of a calendar or school year.

B.2.4   Program conducts at least one face-to-face interview with mentor.

B.2.5   Program conducts a reference check (personal and/or professional) on mentor.

B.2.6   Program conducts a comprehensive criminal background check on adult mentor, including searching a national criminal records database along with sex offender and child abuse registries.

Mentee Screening

B.2.7   Parent(s)/guardian(s) complete an application and provide informed consent for their child to participate.

B.2.8   Parent(s)/guardian(s) and mentee agree to a one (calendar or school) year minimum commitment for the mentoring relationship.

B.2.9   Parents(s)/guardian(s) and mentee agree that the mentee will participate in face-to-face meetings with his or her mentor a minimum of one time per week, on average, for a minimum of one hour per meeting, on average.

Enhancements:

E.2.1   Program utilizes national, fingerprint-based FBI criminal background checks (e.g., the SafetyNET system operating under the auspices of the Child Protection Improvements Act, in cooperation with the National Center for Missing & Exploited Children).

E.2.2   School-based programs assess mentor's interest in maintaining contact with mentee during the summer months following the close of the school year and offer assistance with maintaining contact.

Standard 3: Training

Benchmarks:

Mentor Training

B.3.1   Program provides a minimum of two hours of pre-match, in-person training.

B.3.2   Mentor training includes the following topics, at a minimum: a) Program rules; b) Mentors' goals and expectations for the mentor/mentee relationship; c) Mentors' obligations and appropriate roles; d) Relationship development and maintenance; e) Ethical issues that may arise related to the mentoring relationship; f) Effective closure of the mentoring relationship; and g) Sources of assistance available to support mentors.

Enhancements:

Mentor Training

E.3.1   Program uses evidence-based training materials.

E.3.2   Program provides additional pre-match training opportunities beyond the two-hour, in-person minimum.

E.3.3   Program addresses the following developmental topics in the training: a) Youth development process;

b) Cultural, gender, and economic issues; and c) Opportunities and challenges associated with mentoring specific populations of children (e.g., children of prisoners, youth involved in the juvenile justice system, youth in foster care, high school dropouts), if relevant.

E.3.4   Program uses training to continue to screen mentors for suitability and develops techniques for early trouble-shooting should problems be identified.

Mentee Training

E.3.5   Program provides training for the mentee and his or her parent(s)/guardian(s) (when appropriate) on the following topics: a) Program guidelines; b) Mentors' obligations and appropriate roles; c) Mentees' obligations and appropriate roles; and d) Parental/guardian involvement guidelines.

Standard 4: Matching

Benchmarks:

B.4.1   Program considers its aims, as well as the characteristics of the mentor and mentee (e.g., interests, proximity, availability, age, gender, race, ethnicity, personality, and expressed preferences of mentor and mentee) when making matches.

B.4.2   Program arranges and documents an initial meeting between the mentor and mentee.

Enhancements:

E.4.1   Program staff member should be on site and/or present during the initial meeting of the mentor and mentee.

Standard 5: Monitoring and Support

Benchmarks:

B.5.1   Program contacts the mentor and mentee at a minimum frequency of twice per month for the first month of the match and monthly thereafter.

B.5.2   Program documents information about each mentor-mentee contact, including, at minimum, date, length and nature of contact.

B.5.3   Program provides mentors with access to at least two types of resources (e.g., expert advice from program staff or others; publications; Web-based resources; experienced mentors; available social service referrals) to help mentors negotiate challenges in the mentoring relationships as they arise.

B.5.4   Program follows evidenced-based protocol to elicit more in-depth assessment from the mentor and mentee about the relationship and uses scientifically-tested relationship assessment tools.

B.5.5   Program provides one or more opportunities per year for post-match mentor training.

Enhancements:

E.5.1   Program has quarterly contact with a key person in the mentee's life (e.g., parent, guardian or teacher) for the duration of the match.

E.5.2   Program hosts one or more group activities for mentors and their mentees, and/or offers information about activities that mentors and mentees might wish to participate in together.

E.5.3   Program thanks mentors and recognizes their contributions at some point during each year of the relationship, prior to match closure.

Standard 6: Closure

Benchmarks:

B.6.1   Program has procedure to manage anticipated closures, including a system for a mentor or mentee rematch.

B.6.2   Program has procedure to manage unanticipated match closures, including a system for a mentor or mentee rematch.

B.6.3   Program conducts and documents an exit interview with mentor and mentee.

Enhancements:

E.6.1   Program explores opportunity to continue the mentor/mentee match for a second (or subsequent) year.

E.6.2   Program has a written statement outlining terms of match closure and policies for mentor/mentee contact after a match ends.

E.6.3   Program hosts a final celebration meeting or event with the mentor and mentee to mark progress and transition.

◊   Including the teacher or counselor on Skype calls

◊   Providing specific professional training for prospective mentors

◊   Having a formal list of guidelines for what is, and what isn't, appropriate behavior and conversation. This could include a list of "safe" topics of discussion for mentors and mentees.

Districts should also consider acquiring professional liability insurance in the very unlikely event that participants are accused of inappropriate behavior.

Executive Mentoring

Most mentoring programs focus on students, but there is an emerging trend in setting up mentoring efforts for administrators. (Two are profiled in Section VII, including Florida's PASS Program and Toledo's Principal/Business Mentor Program.) In these partnerships, an experienced manager serves as a mentor to a new principal over the course of a few years, offering their time and expertise (and sometimes funds) to help the administrator tackle tough issues like culture change, goal setting, or time management. Early returns on these efforts have shown impressive results.

Mentor Agreement - Sample

As a volunteer mentor in the (name of your program) Mentoring Program, I agree to:

- Make a one-year commitment to mentoring;

- Attend a training session;

- Be on time for scheduled meetings;

- Notify the program coordinator if I am unable to keep my weekly mentoring session;

- Engage in the relationship with an open mind;

- Accept assistance from my mentee's teacher and/or school support staff;

- Keep discussions with my mentee confidential, unless the child's safety or well-being is at risk or I suspect child abuse;

- Ask program support staff or my business liaison when I need assistance, do not understand something. or am having difficulty with my mentoring relationship;

- Notify the program coordinator of any changes in my employment, address, or telephone number;

- Notify the program coordinator of any significant change in my mentee; and

- Refrain from contacting or seeing my mentee outside of the established parameters and supervised sites where the program takes place.

_____

Signature

_____

Date

Courtesy of The Connecticut Mentoring Partnership, Business Guide to Youth Mentoring, and South Windsor Mentoring Program.

2.4 Real-World Challenges

Real-world challenges and work-based learning are sister approaches: Both provide students with direct exposure to the workplace and/or field operations, professional connections, and a sense of workplace standards. However, there are enough differences to consider them as different partnership models. In work-based learning, the focus is often on the individual experience; real world challenges typically emphasize a team-based approach. Work-based learning often happens in an employer's workplace, while real-world challenges often take place in a school or community setting. Real-world challenges also lend themselves to a project model, with participants focused on reaching some goal. (Work-based learning may or may not be goal-oriented.) And the commitment your partners must make to each is different as well.

A solid, forward-thinking CTE program should include opportunities for real-world experiences for all students. The CTE curriculum itself can be quite challenging and stimulating for students, but the application of that curriculum in a real live business situation brings the curriculum (and learning) to life, deepening the student's understanding and introducing them to real-world expectations and standards. Knowing how the curriculum is applied, and connecting career and technical skills with soft skills such as critical thinking, problem solving, written and oral communications, and working on a team, further deepens the learning process and prepares students for success in college, careers, and life.

Your advisory board members are in a perfect position to provide these real-world opportunities for your students through their own companies and to connect you to others through their networks. By brainstorming with your board members and challenging them to come up with a variety of projects, activities, and real-world experiences, your students can make a great contribution to your partner companies while they are increasing the quality of their learning.

Real-World Partnership Providing Snacks to Diabetic Patients

Dialysis Clinics, Inc., headquartered in Nashville, Tennessee, provides dialysis and other health-care services to patients through 200+ dialysis clinics that serve more than 13,000 patients in 27 states. They are also one of the key partners of Glencliff High School's Academy of Medical Science and Research, which has led to a real-world partnership that provided students with a multifaceted learning opportunity while making a real difference in the lives of DCI patients.

Dialysis patients adhere to a strict diet in order to maintain their health, and one of the common complaints among patients is the lack of tasty snacks or treats. DCI turned to Glencliff's culinary arts program to see if they could find a solution.

Under the guidance of DCI's school partnership coordinator and the head of Glencliff's culinary arts program, students set out to create tasty snacks that fall within the guidelines of diabetic care. Students met with patients, researched dietary requirements and restrictions, created a series of test snacks, and conducted a study to see which ones patients liked best.

After making further modifications based on patient feedback, the students presented a series of snacks that met patient approval and dietary restrictions. DCI has incorporated this effort into their services, and now offer these and similar snacks to patients throughout their service area.

Some examples of real-world challenges/project-based learning might include:

◊ Working with online communications for a partner company, such as designing or updating a website or suggesting ways for a company to take advantage of various social media (Facebook, Twitter, etc.) to expand their marketing efforts.

◊ Having students build a house in collaboration with multiple industry partners, including companies in construction, plumbing, and electrical. In some places, the resulting home is then sold as a fundraiser to fuel the next year's effort. If a house is too large of a project, or too much of a logistical challenge (with travel and site regulations), consider something that smaller that can be on-site, like building and selling sheds or dog houses.

◊ Helping a company's marketing by designing a mobile phone app to help a company market to younger users of their product or service, or making recommendations on a company's logo, brand name, marketing slogan. or other promotion material (newsletters, blogs, advertising campaigns).

◊ Supporting a company's social commitments, such as researching a company's diversity "score" and recommending ways for a company to be more diverse, or examining a company's record for being "eco-friendly" or "green" and making recommendations to the company's management.

◊ Leveraging existing culinary or agriculture programs and providing and/or preparing food for meetings or special events.

◊ Create store displays for seasonal promotions or to promote new fashion lines.

These are just a few examples of how students can get involved in real-world challenges, dealing with issues that businesses face and working side-by-side with them to address those issues. Using the chart below, design a campaign to get your advisory board members and other partners involved in providing real-world challenges (project-based learning experiences) for your students:

Suggested Project	Board Members Who Can Help	Start Date	End Date	Goals of the Project	Goals and Standards to be Met
Design website for company	Company manager who can coordinate with IT department	Xx/xx/xx	Xx/xx/xx	Design a user-friendly website that appeals to younger workforce	Researching, critical thinking, problem solving, oral communications, written communications, presentation skills
Build a new home in the community	General contractor, industry vendors	Xx/xx/xx	Xx/xx/xx	Design and build a house that can be sold to fund next year's program efforts	Design, planning, project management, scheduling, working as a team, resource allocation, numerous technical skills

Other Considerations

As you and your partners plan your real-world challenges, keep the following considerations in mind:

◊ Remember to have students involved in the planning and design phases of a project, and not just in implementation. Planning, scheduling, and project management are key skills they can practice throughout any such project.

◊ Document each phase of your major projects; you can share this with administrators and with future partners to show them what students have accomplished and what they are capable of. Students can use this information as well in their personal portfolios or in college or job applications.

◊ Check with your partner about any workplace restrictions, such as having underaged students on a job site, or having unauthorized personnel in secure areas. You may be limited in what you can do based on workplace safety or security requirements.

◊ Ask your district office about the availability of insurance for students participating in projects off-site. This may or may not be available, and may or may not be required by your partner. Hosting real-world projects at school sites may help you deal with the fact that some workplaces are not able to allow visitors under the age of 18 or 21.

◊ Provide plenty of opportunities for students to work side-by-side with professionals in their area of interest, but follow all standard safety protocols, such as making sure students are not left unsupervised when working with adults.

2.5 Student Work-Based Learning

Student work-based learning activities help to put learning in context, not only in CTE classes, but also in core academic classes. A variety of work-based learning experiences throughout their high school years provides students with opportunities to interact with business leaders, creating "a-ha" moments and often answering the question, "Why do I have to learn this?"

When people talk about work-based learning for students, they're typically talking about a handful of models including job shadowing, internships, and apprenticeships, and they're usually talking about providing opportunities for students in the upper grades. But in reality, there are many ways in which students can learn through exposure to the world outside of school, and these exposures should take place across the high school grades, not just in the final year or two. Think of these options as a continuum or a pipeline: You want students to have experiences across the spectrum in order to get a rounded experience.

The three primary areas to focus on include:

Career Awareness

Career awareness should take place throughout the high school grades with an emphasis in early high school; in fact, career awareness can be extended down as far as the late elementary grades. A work-based learning approach to career awareness should include basic exposure to the business world, including guest speakers from different lines of work and different industries; visiting different businesses to get a sense of what companies do and how they operate; and getting a "wide scan" of the many different types of careers out there and the many different paths to entering various fields.

Career Exploration

In career exploration, students move beyond their initial scans of the work world and start to learn some of the details of various professions, such as the required skill set, educational path, working environment, and day-to-day tasks. Students will focus on a deeper dive into specific careers that interest them, including spending more time in the field via job shadowing, and start to gather the kind of information that will allow them to make informed choices.

Career Preparation and Application

This is what many consider to be traditional work-based learning: Students actively working in a field through internships and apprenticeships. But even this phase can include other activities, such as more intensive preparation and planning for various postsecondary paths and an even deeper learning effort through tools such as career mentors.

Work-Based Learning Worksheet

The following chart provides a sample of work-based learning activities that can be considered during students' four years of high school. Put an "X" in the columns for the grades for which you may consider these activities for your students.

Grade / Work-Based Learning Activities	9th grade	10th grade	11th grade	12th grade
Career Awareness				
Accompany parent to work — then report out to class				
Attend career fair				
Bring in classroom speakers — both industry and postsecondary options				
Review industry/career information online				
Visit a college class				
Do a workplace tour of a local business				
Participate in a meeting of your chamber of commerce, industry council, or trade union				
Bring your parent to school day				
Work on a project with a board member to determine what careers go with what the student is interested in (ex: animals > veterinarian)				
Career Exploration				
Job shadow				
Bring in industry expert speakers				
Research career options online within an industry/profession				
Identify colleges that offer career courses in which student is interested				
Research your own interests, talents, skills, and abilities; identify career paths that require/capitalize on these attributes; look at the postsecondary requirements of each				
Visit with chamber of commerce members to explore industries/career opportunities in region/state				
Attend a career fair at a college or company or in the community				
Attend an industry trade show or conference				
Career Preparation and Application				
Research college degrees and/or industry certifications required for a successful career				
Attend a career fair at a college or company or in the community				
Find career mentors for students				
Secure a paid internship or apprenticeship for every student				
Connect business partners and students in resume writing/mock interview exercises				
Attend "new employee orientation" meetings at business partners' companies				
Visit college campuses — interview college students whose majors/career goals are connected to program's theme				
Bring counselors into classroom to discuss college application/financial aid processes				
Complete college applications/financial aid applications				

The chart on the previous page provides a sample of work-based learning activities that can be considered during the students' four years of high school. Put an "X" in the column for the grade for which you may consider these activities for your students, and be sure to involve your existing partners and advisory board members as volunteer participants, coaches, hosts, and leaders.

Additional Thoughts

◊ Remember that work-based learning experiences can occur in the classroom as well as outside of school in the workplace and in the community. If travel is an issue, look for opportunities to bring work-based learning opportunities to you.

◊ Try to offer students a variety of workplace tours and job-shadowing opportunities; this gives them a better sense of what is available to them and allows them to better target their future exploration efforts.

◊ Don't send students into a job-shadowing or internship opportunity unless they're prepared to act appropriately. This may mean a few days of instruction and practice on workplace behavior (dress, showing up on time, etc.).

◊ Internships should be reserved for older students who are more mature and who have gained enough experience to know that a field is of interest to them.

2.6 Teacher Learning Experiences

It's not uncommon for teachers, particularly those in CTE, to have gotten their start in the business world. And those teachers come to the classroom with a certain grounding in industry that they can pass along to their students, providing more relevance to what they're teaching in the classroom and helping students make important connections.

But if those teachers don't maintain regular contact with their industries, it's possible that they'll lose that business orientation, and they'll certainly lose touch with current knowledge, practices, equipment, and changes in the market as time goes by. And for those teachers who have never had significant exposure to industry (including many in general subject areas), it is doubly challenging to bring that perspective and knowledge into the classroom.

Whether teachers began their careers in industry or not, they benefit greatly from interacting with the business community. Some of that exposure can come from inviting the business community into the classroom, such as hosting guest speakers or bringing in businesspeople to work with students as mentors or project coaches. But teachers also benefit strongly from direct interaction, either informally or through workplace-based interactions. A few examples:

◊ Business partners can provide your teachers with current resources from the field, such as recent trade journals, materials from conferences, and training videos.

◊ Partners regularly train their employees on new equipment and practices; they may be willing to invite your teachers to participate.

◊ Similarly, their staff members may be available to train your staff on various job functions, either on-site or at your school.

◊ Some businesses and business coalitions have set up summer internship programs for teachers, giving them a full week or two weeks at the workplace to get an immersive experience in the field. Many of these programs encourage teachers to write one or more lesson plans based on their experiences, and some encourage the employees with whom they worked to visit teachers' classrooms to support the lesson.

Additional Thoughts

◊ Ask your teachers what their interests are in industry-related professional development, and use that to make connections.

◊ Ask board members and other partners to keep you regularly informed of changes in their markets, particularly as they might relate to your programs. Share that information with teachers, and see whether your partners can offer opportunities to keep your teachers current.

2.7 Advocacy

Strictly speaking, advocacy is not a partnership model: As an educator, there's actually little you can do as an active partner while your business counterparts advocate for your work. But it is a critically important way in which businesses can support your program, and it something that you can encourage and facilitate behind the scenes.

Advocacy Among Community Leaders

The business partner voice can be a powerful ally if your program's future is threatened in some way, or when your program needs a special level or type of support. Some examples of challenges and opportunities include:

◊ Maintaining program visibility and importance in the face of a change in leadership at the building or district level

◊ Dealing with changes in district or federal funding

◊ Passing a new bond issue

◊ Lobbying a political leader to support funding

◊ Raising awareness at the district or state DOE level

◊ Building the profile of your program among the business community, including attracting new partners and donors

When your advisory board members are passionate about their involvement, they become very selfish about your program's future health and existence. And no matter what the threat or opportunity, your advisory board members and other critical partners can often make a much stronger case for your program's continuation than you may be able to make on your own.

Board members and other business partners can attend school board meetings to argue on behalf of your program. They may also have a "louder" voice in meetings with the superintendent, principal and/or core academic staff, as well as with local and state political figures. It's quite likely that none of your community leaders wish to upset the business community, and if your business partners truly believe in the efficacy and sustainability of your program, then their voice may become the strongest vote to keep your program open and funded.

Advocacy with Students and Parents

In addition to advocating among political, district, and business stakeholders, your partners can also advocate for your program among students and parents. Sometimes, you'll just want their help in making potential students aware of the benefits of your program. In some cases, parents are concerned that a career-focused program may pigeon-hole a student, and limit that student's vision as to his/her college and career opportunities. Business partners can speak to parents about the new Three R's of your program, focusing on the "holistic" approach taken by the combination of a rigorous curriculum, relevant work-based learning experiences, and important, often life-long networking relationships. The impact of these Three R's, and your business partners' voices carrying the message, may help improve enrollment in and the sustainability of your program.

Resource Support

Finally, it is not unusual for even well-funded programs to require additional funding for supplies, trips, or scholarships. This is when your business partners can step up and make a pitch to a variety of sources to provide the additional funding required. Business partners may advocate for increased funding for your program from the district, the state, the federal government, from their own companies, from the chamber of commerce, from local private and corporate foundations and other non-profit sources, and from the community at large. In this way, business partners can be a pivotal financial resource for your program.

Don't Lead with Advocacy

Advocacy provides significant benefits for your program, and your partners do benefit by being a visible part of a winning team (not to mention the thrill of victory!). But you should remember that every time your partners advocate for your program, they're sticking their necks out a bit, leveraging their reputations and relationships for your benefit. For this reason, you should only expect support in this area from board members and partners who have worked with you for some time, who have knowledge of your program and confidence in your abilities, and who feel like a real part of your team. You cannot expect first-time partners to go out into the community to speak on your behalf: You have to earn their trust and build the relationship before they'll be willing to advocate for you.

Finally, don't expect an open-ended advocacy effort: Campaigns work better when there's a goal and a limited time window, such as a bond campaign or a fundraising drive. This allows partners to expend a burst of energy in a short time frame and see the results of their efforts.

2.8 Resource Support

Since the start of public education, business partners have offered financial support, goods, and services to support instruction and provide students with more opportunity. In the past, this was viewed by most businesspeople as a charitable activity; today, however, educators need to look at it through the same return oninvestment (ROI) lens that they use to consider other partnership models.

What this means is that a relationship based solely on donations is probably going to be a weak partnership: Your partner will receive only limited benefits from the effort, and you won't receive the levels of support from that partner that you might see from a deeper relationship. You and your partner will see much greater returns if you start by looking at other types of partnership models, and consider resource support as a second-stage, or supporting, model.

As an example, think about the role of businesses in the FIRST Robotics Competition. Teams welcome any sort of financial support, but the primary push from FIRST is to get businesspeople involved as volunteers or mentors. They understand that deeper relationships help businesspeople feel like part of the team and see firsthand what kind of an impact the program has on students. Donors generally aren't engaged in that way, and as a result, their support may not be as deep or lasting.

That said, there is a definite role for donations within your school or program. Some organizations, like corporate foundations, can only provide financial donations, while some partners want to provide direct incentives to students, such as scholarships or prizes, as part or all of their commitment. And for some, it just makes sense to provide support in the form of the goods they produce or the services they provide.

Resource Support: Don't Limit Your Thinking!

When people talk about donations, their thoughts usually go directly to financial donations, scholarships, support for at-risk students (such as food drives or backpack programs), or commonly used items in the classroom like raw materials for CTE classes. But almost any kind of donation can make an impact on your program, either by replacing something that you previously had to pay for, or by improving the instructional experience.

Consider the work of the Simon Property Group, which owns or manages some of the most prominent mall properties in America. After seeing the impact it could achieve by reaching youth through mall-driven initiatives, corporate leaders developed a strategy to leverage unused mall space to house non-traditional public schools that serve at-risk students who may homeless, gravely ill, working full time to support their families, or otherwise unable to attend a traditional high school.

Mall leaders present the opportunity to their local school boards; if approved, the mall provides free space for the school and agrees to invest up to $350,000 to build out the space to make it an appropriate learning environment. They also agree to refresh each site on a five-year schedule (new paint, carpet, etc.). School districts cover utilities (often at a discounted rate), furnishings, and staff. The company's nonprofit arm, Simon Youth Foundation, also offers professional development opportunities to teachers and scholarships to students. Mall leaders also work to establish work-based learning opportunities with local businesses, both inside and outside the mall.

As of 2013, there are 23 Simon Youth Academies in 13 states. Sites boast a 90 percent graduation rate, with more than 10,000 at-risk students earning their high school diplomas. And more than $10 million in scholarships has been awarded to some 3,300 students in 42 states.

Some tips on handling donated resources, so that you and your partners benefit as greatly as possible:

◊ Try to avoid having financial donations go into the general school fund; while everyone has the best of intentions, it becomes easy for those funds to be diverted away from their intended purpose, and you rarely

The Danger of Dollars: A Cautionary Tale

Financial gifts, while always welcome, are not always the answer to the problems facing a program or a school: Without careful planning and strong stewardship, those dollars may well leave little trace after they're gone. The Annenberg Challenge illustrates that point well.

On a cold, blustery day in December 1993, Walter J. Annenberg, founder and publisher of TV Guide, stood with President Bill Clinton at the White House to announce the Annenberg Challenge, a donation of $500 million intended to reform the public education system. It was widely acknowledged to be the largest gift to public schools in history up to that point.

Annenberg's funds were to be distributed over a five year period through four primary initiatives: gifts to nine major urban school districts, support for a consortium of rural schools, grants to two national reform organizations, and gifts to a collection of arts education projects in New York and elsewhere.

The money was not given to the schools themselves: instead, it was distributed to intermediary groups in each market that would oversee how the funds were spent based on strategies developed locally. To ensure a commitment on the part of those communities, each was required to secure matching funds, bringing the total collective contribution to $1.1 billion.

What resulted from the Annenberg Challenge is widely considered to be — at best — a disappointment. Local groups largely treated the problems in K–12 education as a resource issue, and sent a surge of funds into existing district programs. The result, noted one of the evaluators, is that "the school districts and the schools gobbled up those grants like lunch and they were ready for the next one."

While these funds were accompanied by bold language about real reform, the requirements themselves encouraged local organizations to skirt confrontational approaches. The Challenge encouraged the independent organizations receiving support to negotiate change with the existing actors, mandating that participating schools and districts sign off on any plans before proceeding.

Some of the larger urban partnerships involved the following kinds of strategies:

New York
The Annenberg project in New York relied on the collaborative efforts of four different organizations with complementary, but not identical, interests and approaches to education reform, and required that they share authority for the use of the funds. The project had a small schools model at its core, and had a stated desire to prove this model and replicate it (in a range of forms) across the city. According to independent reports, there were some modest improvements in outcomes among some participating schools, but change did not spread, nor was it sustained.

Philadelphia
This site was the only one to attempt to redesign the entire district of 257 schools. The goals of the project were sweeping, with a range of initiatives including incorporating new technology, improving professional development, enhancing assessment models, improving attendance rates, building the image of the district, and increasing community services for students. Funds somehow flowed into the district's general budget and were not tracked in terms of their application to fulfilling these objectives. According to evaluators, many indicators of student performance improved over the course of the grant implementation, but there was no expectation that gains would be sustained once funding ended.

Chicago
In Chicago, the local grantmaking body focused on school "networks," which contained at least three schools and a community partner, and also encouraged small school models. Small grants were doled out to several schools, but the application process was complicated, and the range of models all but ensured that any reforms could not be tracked and replicated across the district. Furthermore, as the Chicago plan was being implemented, other major changes were taking place in the district, and no one has been able to ascertain whether any improvements in the district could be attributed to the Annenberg grant.

While these programs were able to serve more students and undoubtedly made some kind of difference at the time, there were no lasting changes in the broader school and district environments. Once the money had all been spent, there was very little to indicate that the grants had ever been made.

As a result, according to Michael Casserly of the Council of Great City Schools, "The best I can say about Annenberg was that it provided us a terrific bad example. The grants were poorly conceived, poorly managed, and ... disconnected from any ability to drive broader policy changes. The lesson is: Don't do that again."

have any recourse once that happens. You can work with an outside organization, like an education foundation, to accept those funds and use them as directed, or you can ask your partner to purchase the needed resources and donate those directly.

◊   Make specific requests. Instead of saying you need auto shop supplies, say you need a case of oil, or a complete set of tools, or a late-model car. That way supporters will understand how their resources are being used, and will have the satisfaction of filling a request. You can also request support for a specific activity, such as student travel to a competition.

◊   It's good to ask for what you need, but be prepared to accept and use items that are easiest for your partner to provide. Remember that donated resources mean you don't have to use funds in that area, freeing them up to address your highest needs. Remember also that even if you don't have a need for the donation, another teacher might be extremely grateful for the support, and may help you find what you need in the future. It might be helpful to assemble a school-wide list of resource needs, which would help you avoid duplicating efforts.

◊   If several of your programs have common needs, or even if identical programs at different sites have the same needs, consider banding

---

Sample Donation Receipt Letter

Date

Name
Title
Company
Address
City, State, Zip

Dear First Name,

Thank you very much for providing our Aviation Program with access to your flight simulator! As you know, our goal is to provide students with real-world connections to the industry, and having access to a resource like yours that's used in training pilots professionally is going to make a significant contribution to our students' success.

The time that students have spent with your simulator is already changing their lives. Bill Wilson, who you met during our first trip to your facility, has decided to pursue a career in the field and has already signed up for classes at the community college in the fall. When I talked with him about his plans, he specifically mentioned his experience with your simulator as a deciding factor.

We appreciate your support of our students, and we would welcome opportunities to work with you further. We rely on industry professionals like you to serve as guest speakers and mentors and to provide internships for students ready to take a next step on their path toward the industry. If you would like to share your time, just let me know.

Again, thank you for all you do for our kids.

Sincerely,

Malcolm Wexter
Executive Director

together in a "clearinghouse" model. Many districts and education foundations have done this for general classroom supplies: "Teacher Warehouses" are popular in many markets. Work with other educators to establish a single contact and let your partners know about your common needs; it's much better than having 10 programs asking the same partner for the same things.

◊ Ask your partners if their vendors can support your work. Each year, the nonprofit Share Our Strength hosts "Taste of the Nation" events in cities across the country, and donates 100 percent of ticket proceeds from these celebrations of local restaurants. They're able to do so because all of the local restaurants participating in the event ask their vendors to donate the food for the night, which they do in order to maintain good relationships with the restaurants. Your partner's vendors may be just as interested in helping you in order to maintain good relationships with their clients.

The Thank You Letter

It's important to thank your donors in writing: In addition to the fact that a thank you letter is good manners, your donors may be able to use your letter for tax purposes, and you may be able to secure future support as a result.

When writing your letter, be sure to thank your donor by name, referring to the specific gift (no form letters!), reinforcing the connection to your program, and telling them how the gift was used. You can then invite your donor to participate in your program in some other way, such as volunteering, serving as a guest speaker, or advising in some area of interest to them. See the sample letter in this section for more.

2.9 Program Start-Up or Retrofit

NOTE: *The team you build to assist with a program start-up or retrofit will use many of the same approaches and tools as your program's ongoing advisory board. Employer Engagement Toolkit devotes an entire section to advisory boards (Section VI, "Deep Dive: Advisory Boards"); look there for helpful resources.*

Most CTE program leaders are familiar with the purpose and many functions of the advisory board. But in times of dramatic change, such as when a new industry emerges and needs a CTE program to support it, or when an existing industry sees major developments, an advisory board might not be the best vehicle for navigating that change. In those cases, you may need to undergo a formal program start-up or retrofit in order to quickly identify industry needs and build a program to match. This requires a different advisory structure and action steps before you can move to a more management-minded advisory board oversight model.

The key differences between the start-up/retrofit model and the advisory model include differences in scope, intensity, and time frames. Start-ups and retrofits needs to have a much broader focus on the industry landscape, and have the leeway to consider many options in responding to business needs. The work is more intensive, but takes place for a short time, between three and 12 months. Once the new program structure is in place, then you'll be able to manage it using a traditional advisory board.

Options

◊ When the need for a new program becomes apparent, gather a working group of industry representatives in the new or changing field. This group should identify the following information:

» Current jobs in this industry within the region.

» Prospective job growth in this industry sector based on non-proprietary projections of company expansion and industry trends.

» Average wages and benefits for jobs within the industry sector.

» The knowledge and skill sets that are needed for jobs in the industry sector.

» Relevant industry certifications that exist for jobs within the industry sector.

◊ When the working group has gathered its data, members should begin scheduling appointments with numerous stakeholders, including the district's CTE coordinator, the superintendent, and members of the school board. Committee members should also meet with stakeholders from relevant local postsecondary programs. In each of these meetings, members can share the information they've gathered and ask if there are any current programs that address some or all of the skill sets called for in your industry sector.

◊ While some or most of your working committee will transition to the new program's advisory board, make it clear that the working committee is a temporary structure. This will help to set expectations among members, letting them know that the committee requires only a limited commitment (though the work may be intensive during that time).

Additional Thoughts

◊ When business partners want to start a new program or significantly retrofit an existing program, they should proceed with urgency, but also with an understanding of the education decision-making process. Build and maintain goodwill between business partners and existing teachers and school staff. Business partners should know that change is possible but that there is a process that schools must follow and that the process may take longer than it would in private industry, as teachers and school leaders are subject to policy and funding decisions made by the school board.

◊ Further, in a tight fiscal environment, new program funding may require reallocation of resources, a process that can create opposition. From the education perspective, a CTE coordinator or other administrator will need to be an internal champion, working with the various decision-making bodies and navigating rules, regulations, and budget issues. This person should stay in close contact with one lead representative for the business partners, keeping them informed of the process, next steps, and when more external participation is needed.

◊ If the business partners can bring resources to the table in terms of volunteers, equipment, and direct funding, that will speak clearly to the potential value of the new or refurbished program.

How to Recruit Partners

EET

3.1 Different Kinds of Business Partners

When you think about partnering with the business community, it helps to remember that you're not just targeting one kind of organization: There are different sizes and types of businesses, and they each have different motivations, resources, and approaches to working with schools.

Large Businesses, Including National/International Firms

There are definite advantages to working with large companies: They can bring significant resources to your program, they bring a level of credibility to projects they get involved in, and they can influence stakeholders (civic leaders, other businesspeople) on your behalf. However, you may have to work through some bureaucratic channels to make the partnership happen: It may be difficult to find the right people to talk to, and they may have rules about how they work with schools (many large companies funnel their resources into "signature programs").

◊ **Headquarters** – If you're fortunate enough to have the headquarters of a large business in your community, or perhaps even in your state, you may have access to the best of both worlds: Ample resources with the discretion to pioneer new approaches. However, you may face challenges based on how the company is set up, for example, if the company's headquarters is just a small central office and most of the hands-on work (particularly work that might align with CTE programs) is handled elsewhere. In these cases, it may be best to look for support in the form of resources.

◊ **Regional or Satellite Office** – While still a powerfully ally, non-headquarters locations will probably have to follow guidelines set elsewhere, so be sure to find out what those guidelines are. In some businesses, remote sites have the freedom to experiment, with the best ideas "migrating up" to the central office, so you may still have opportunities for innovation.

◊ **US Office of an International Firm** – Foreign firms with a US presence may be particularly interesting prospects. Other countries handle education differently than we do; vocational training is a recognized

---

Case in Point: Siemens

Germany is one of several European countries with a strong cultural commitment to vocational education: A large percentage of firms participate in workforce development initiatives at the secondary and postsecondary levels, offering students exposure to the workplace and preparing them through participation in the classroom and through internships and apprenticeships.

Siemens, an international advanced manufacturing firm headquartered in Germany, took the practices of its home country and has begun applying them in the United States. Its Charlotte, North Carolina, location has joined a local consortium called Apprenticeship 2000 and began offering apprenticeships to students identified through the consortium in 2011. Students are full-time students at the local community college (Central Piedmont Community College, or CPCC), and by the time they have completed the apprenticeship program, they will have earned a degree in mechatronics engineering and also have a full-time position with Siemens.

career track, and businesses there are active participants in the preparation of young people with internships, apprenticeships, and other types of involvement. US branches of those firms may be more open to deeper and different levels of involvement in your program.

If you don't have an existing entry point into a large local headquarters, start by approaching someone in their community relations office; they can explore opportunities through internal channels and connect you with the right people.

Corporate Foundations

Many large and mid-sized businesses have a corporate foundation; these may or may not be directly connected to the work that the company does. A bank's foundation, for example, may target issues like financial literacy, or they may deal with social issues not related to finance at all. You may find the foundation to be an independent organization, but in many cases, it is managed by the corporate citizenship office. Most only offer funding through grants, but some, particularly those run by the company itself, may also connect applicants to volunteers as part of the resources they provide.

If the foundation doesn't maintain its own website, either on its own or as part of the company's community relations section, you can get more information by looking them up on GuideStar (www.GuideStar.org) or at The Foundation Center (www.foundationcenter.org).

Self-Assessment:

List one or two of your most important partners in each of the categories below and answer the following questions:

Large Business: _____

Small Business: _____

Business Coalition: _____

- ◊ *How did you connect with them in the beginning? Were there differences among the categories?*

- ◊ *What do they contribute to your partnerships? Are some more likely to contribute funds, volunteers, expertise, or workplace experiences?*

- ◊ *Why do they partner with you? Are their motivations different as a group?*

Mid-Sized Businesses (100–500 employees)

Mid-sized businesses tend to be local or regional enterprises, meaning that they have more resources than a small business but are still able to focus entirely on local efforts (unlike large national companies that may need to spread their support around). They often have some flexibility, but you'll also likely need to work through a somewhat bureaucratic process; you'll probably be working with department heads and community representatives, and not with owners or executive managers. Mid-sized firms can be excellent partners because they usually have a large enough workforce to allow for numerous adult/student relationships, and the facilities needed to conduct workplace tours and host apprentices and interns.

Small Businesses (up to 100 employees)

Small businesses are often your most flexible partners. You'll often end up working directly with the ultimate decision-maker — an owner who can make decisions and commit resources without needing approval from a committee. While they may not be able to provide the levels of resources and opportunities that the largest employers can offer, they can do quite a bit, and as a group they serve as the foundation of many programs across the country. They're also very accessible, either through business coalition contacts or through direct outreach.

Business Coalitions

Business coalitions can be powerful partners, providing a single point of contact for dozens or even hundreds of businesses in your community. Workforce preparedness is usually one of their top priorities, and programs that can produce skilled and prepared employees are of great interest.

Note that there are different types of business groups:

◊ **Workforce Investment Boards, or WIBs** – WIBs focus on helping the unemployed and underemployed find good jobs. Some only serve adults, while others express an interest in the workers of the future.

◊ **Economic Development Corporations, or EDCs** – EDCs are most interested in attracting employers and other assets to their communities. The quality of their local workforce is a top selling point.

◊ **Industry Sector Groups** – These are local or regional organizations that work to advance the interests of a single industry sector, focusing on lobbying, sharing best practices, and advocating for a strong workforce.

◊ **Chambers of Commerce** – Chambers are networking and advocacy organizations that represent the multiple needs of businesses within a geographic area. Workforce preparedness is a primary concern.

The best strategy is to get involved in your local coalitions: join, attend meetings, and/or get involved in appropriate committees and events. On a program level, you can make contacts who can benefit your program by providing guest speakers, student and teacher learning opportunities, and more. And on a broader level, you can help these coalitions understand the challenges faced in education and work together to address them.

3.2 Where to Find Partners

One of the biggest challenges in partnership development is finding partners to work with. Most people feel uncomfortable making cold calls, and educators are no exception, so we put off that outreach work as long as we can. As a result, year after year, most schools fail to see the kinds of results that a vibrant base of partners can provide.

There's good news, however. Partnership development doesn't have to mean making cold calls all day: The key is to make "warm calls," which just means taking advantage of existing connections to build your new relationships. By focusing on warm calls, you and your future partners will already have something in common, like a mutual contact or a shared interest, which will serve as a jumping-off point for your discussion.

Developing a Target List

Before you get out there, however, you need to develop a plan. Yes, you want partners — but which ones? Who are your best partnership prospects? Who's most likely to want to work with you, and have the resources to do so?

You can identify many of your best potential partners by doing a little research. There are organizations in your city, region, and state that can identify the largest and fastest-growing companies, often broken out by industry sector, providing you with an excellent starting point. The types of organizations may vary from one community to the next, but most often, you're looking for your chamber of commerce or an EDC.

The Economic Development Directory (www.ecodevdirectory.com) is a good place to start; while this is not a comprehensive resource, it does offer a very good starting point, allowing you to search for all relevant organizations by state and then by region. You'll want to add to your search by reaching out to your local chamber and identifying any relevant industry sector organizations in your market. You may also find innovation hubs by talking with your postsecondary contacts.

Doing research through these channels will provide you with a strong initial list of the largest and fastest-growing companies in your area. But remember that it's only a starting point: There are any number of small businesses that may not show up on these lists but will make excellent partners. So as you start to reach out, let people know that you'd like inroads into the major companies you identified, but that you're also very interested in their suggestions as well.

Tapping Into Your Personal Network

No matter how few business connections you currently have, your existing network of relationships can take you much farther than you might expect.

Consider the following opportunities:

Your Fellow Teachers and Administrators

Every one of the teachers in your building, whether in CTE or not, has contacts in the business world who might be interested in the work you're doing. It may be a professional contact, like another CTE teacher's business partner, who may know people in your field; it may be another teacher's wife or brother-in-law. But the first place to start would be to talk with your fellow educators about your desire to connect with businesspeople, and ask them to work through their contact files to see what kinds of introductions they can make. It may make sense to bring all your CTE teachers together on a regular basis to share connections, and for targeted STEM programs, to also invite your science and math teachers.

Self-Assessment:

List three of your fellow educators who might be able to introduce you to possible business partners:

Educator 1: _____

Educator 2: _____

Educator 3: _____

Vendors

You and your administrators deal with many vendors to supply your programs with needed materials. If you're buying the same kinds of materials that businesses in your field are buying, then the odds are that your vendors are also selling to businesses in your industry and in your area. Tell your vendors what you're looking for and ask if they know of anyone they can introduce you to; this would give them a chance to help out two customers at once! As a bonus, you can ask them for insights into who the largest and fastest-growing businesses are in your area, giving you some very helpful market intelligence as you go forward.

Self-Assessment:

List three vendors who might be able to introduce you to possible business partners:

Vendor 1: _____

Vendor 2: _____

Vendor 3: _____

Current Partners, Volunteers, and Guest Speakers

Even if you don't have all of the partners you want, you probably have at least a handful of active and committed businesspeople who have already bought into your program. Whether these are CEOs or individual businesspeople serving as mentors or volunteers, they all understand firsthand what you're doing and can serve as excellent ambassadors when reaching out to their peers.

Self-assessment:

List three of your current partners who might be able to introduce you to new business partners:

Partner 1: _____

Partner 2: _____

Partner 3: _____

Advisory Board Members

Advisory boards serve as a window for your program into the community, and a window for the community into your program. One of your advisory board members' core functions is therefore to let others know what you're doing and ask them to join the effort.

There are two factors here: First, whether you've recruited the right people to your board — specifically, that at least a few of them have professional networks that you can access — and second, whether you've actually asked them to help you make those connections. Assuming these are both true, your board should be serving as a powerful source of introductions into the business community. In addition to asking for help at one of your advisory board meetings, you might also consider making the partner recruiting function a formal role for your board, making it clear that it's one of the job responsibilities of board members, or even setting up a committee devoted to partnership development.

Parents

Parents are an often-overlooked component of your network. But if you've had a chance to get to know them, you know that some may be well-connected in the community; in fact, some may even work at the companies on your target list! And of course they have a powerful motivation to see your program succeed.

Self-Assessment:

List three parents who might be able to introduce you to possible business partners:

Parent 1: _____

Parent 2: _____

Parent 3: _____

Postsecondary Partners

Many secondary-level CTE programs have active relationships with educators at their local community colleges, whether formal (such as articulation agreements or dual credit arrangements) or informal. These educators have their own networks of businesses within your shared industry sector and will likely see the value in helping their partners connect with students at the secondary level. As noted in Section VI (Advisory Boards), it may even be helpful to explore the idea of shared advisory boards between secondary and postsecondary programs.

Self-Assessment:

List three of your current partners who might be able to introduce you to new business partners:

Partner 1: _____

Partner 2: _____

Partner 3: _____

Former Students

Have you kept in touch with any students after they've graduated? You'll likely find that at least some of them have pursued a career in your field, possibly even working at some of your target companies. And who would be in a better position to represent the value of your program to a prospective partner, than a valued employee who you introduced to the industry? If you don't currently have relationships with former students, start working now to stay in touch with current students as they graduate; it will be rewarding for you both.

Self-Assessment:

List three of your former students who might be able to introduce you to new business partners:

Student 1: _____

Student 2: _____

Student 3: _____

Personal Interests

You have a life outside of school, whether it's involvement in your church, a civic group, charitable work, an athletic league, or all of the above. Each of these activities puts you in touch with people you would not have otherwise met, and who have personal and professional networks of their own. As you talk casually with others in your groups, you may find some new inroads into your target list or learn about other companies that might be a good fit for your program — there's no harm at all in asking for a little help in making that connection.

Self-assessment:

List three of your personal connections who might be able to introduce you to new business partners:

Connection 1: _____

Connection 2: _____

Connection 3: _____

Detroit's Education Engagement Project

It's no secret that the city of Detroit is facing significant challenges. However, those who believe that education in Detroit is a lost cause would be wrong: There are still many islands of success to be found, and the schools that are doing the hard work of effectively educating their students are benefiting from community support through programs such as the Education Engagement Project (EEP).

Like many other business groups, the Detroit Regional Chamber of Commerce had worked for years to support local education efforts. According to Greg Handel, senior director of workforce development, "What we've found is that if we approach a school that's not performing well, thinking that we can fix that from the outside by providing resources, the results have been disappointing. We've learned that if a school is not academically achieving, there are often deeper issues than resources. But what we can do is look for schools that are moving in the right direction and work with them. This was a big change in thinking for us."

The Detroit Chamber saw this as an area in which it could provide value and in 2006 launched EEP. EEP helps to establish business/education partnerships for schools that have been moving in a positive direction. They do this by encouraging chamber members to work with selected schools, and training schools on how to work with business partners.

EEP began by conducting school tours for members of the business community. Through these tours, business leaders had an opportunity to sit down and talk with parents, students, and school leaders to learn about the school from the perspective of multiple stakeholders.

An important step in this process, according to Chamber liaison Brooke Franklin, involves preparing principals for these site visits. "We took the time to go sit down with these principals and help them understand how to tell their stories," said Franklin. "They need to be able to articulate how they got from where they were to where they are today. It wasn't about putting up a front: You can see through that in a second. It was about presenting their actual work and accomplishments, showcasing what they're already doing to create change."

The tours had a powerful impact: Many business leaders would actually double back to talk further with the schools without even being asked by the chamber about next steps. This enthusiasm came in part from the fact that businesspeople were so impressed by the leadership and practices that they found in place at selected schools, and they were excited to have a chance to help advance the efforts of people who were already doing a lot of things right.

As business and school leaders began working together, EEP saw a variety of partnerships being put into place. It was important to EEP that the education and business partners decided themselves on the scope and type of the partnership so the partners could find the right fit for them.

While EEP continues to conduct tours, they're finding that current business partners are now bringing others to the table through word of mouth. The chamber also promotes partnership opportunities through their website, publications, and meetings.

Going forward, EEP plans on expanding the level of support they provide to business and education leaders. No matter what they do, however, it will be based on the premise that good partnerships will only take place when building on a solid foundation.

Taking Advantage of Networking Organizations

Up to this point, we've looked at maximizing your own personal and professional networks to make industry contacts. But there are also organizations that exist in large part to help you make these kinds of connections, and educators who get involved in these groups can see significant benefits.

You've already looked to your chamber of commerce, economic development organizations, and other groups as a source of information in learning about the industry landscape. But information is just one of the values that these groups offer; another lies in connecting their members to one another.

Go back and look at that list of connector organizations again. Do they accept memberships? Do they have committees that would be relevant to you, such as an industry-specific committee, or one focused on education or workforce issues? Do they have general gatherings or special events that you can attend?

Some tips for getting the most out of these organizations:

◊ It's not enough to pay your membership dues: You've got to be active in the organization, attending meetings and serving on committees. If you don't get involved, you'll get very little benefit.

◊ Be a constructive member of the organization. Members may have had bad experiences with the education system, or have an unfounded bias against it. Rather than act as an apologist, acknowledge their concerns and redirect the conversation in a more positive direction, looking at what can be done to address issues going forward rather than defending things you likely had no connection with.

◊ Ask one of the organization's staff members for help. Let them know that you're there to learn what issues the business community is facing, but also that you're interested in finding new partners to support your work. If the organization is interested in workforce issues, they'll likely be very interested in helping you.

◊ Ask if you can host a general meeting, or at least a committee meeting, at your school. Be prepared to give attendees a tour of your programs, highlighting your successes and the value your program provides to local workforce preparedness efforts.

3.3 What to Look for in a Partner

Educators appreciate all those who are willing to contribute to the success of their students. But there are certain characteristics that point to a high-value partner: An organization or an individual who has the potential to make a significant contribution to your work, and with whom you can build a long-term relationship. And there are ways you can purposefully look for the kinds of people best qualified to fuel your work.

Ideal Qualities of a Business Partner

While all of your partners will have at least some of these, it's the partners who carry most or all with them that you really want to pursue.

A Focus on the Students

First and foremost, every partner has to have a sincere interest in providing students with opportunities that engage them, expand their horizons, and help them develop into adults (as workers and as people). It's fine for partners to also have personal motives (see below), but this focus on the students is a must.

A Clear Benefit for Themselves

Partners must also have a clear sense of what's in it for them. If they don't perceive a real benefit from being involved with your school, their initial enthusiasm may fade in favor of more rewarding opportunities. Of course, if they don't come in with a clear sense of their return on investment (ROI), you can help them identify their ROI using the information in Section 1.

Time

Partnering with schools requires that businesses commit some amount of time to the effort. This may be extensive (as in volunteering programs) or not, but at a minimum your partners need to take the time to gain firsthand knowledge about the work you're doing. Be aware that some people may have a tendency to overcommit.

Resources

Resources don't have to be financial in nature: They can involve the time of mentors or volunteers, they may include the expertise that your partners bring to your advisory board or student competitions, or they may be reflected in your partners' advocacy efforts. But for a partnership to exist, each party — including your business partner — must bring something of value to the relationship.

A Collaborative Approach

Interpersonal skills, like having a positive attitude and considering other peoples' points of view, are extremely important in developing a long-lasting relationship. The assets a partner brings to a project can be alluring, but at the end of the day, this is someone you're going to spend time with on a regular basis.

Reliability

There are few things worse than inviting students to an exciting special event, only to have your partner show up unprepared — or worse, to not show up at all! If you're going to trust businesses to work with your staff and students, they must be dependable, able to fulfill any commitments they make.

Understanding

Education and business can be very different environments; education often requires more consensus-building and may involve specific approval processes, for example. Partnerships go much more smoothly when your business partners understand and accommodate those differences.

Finding Partners that Meet Your Needs

As Stephen R. Covey said in his *Seven Habits of Highly Effective People*, "Begin with the End in Mind." As you begin the task of recruiting business partners, think about any particular needs facing your programs or your students. Do you need people who are good at fundraising? How about people who can provide or find paid internships for your students? Do you need someone with excellent leadership skills to be your advisory board chair? What about someone who has excellent presentation skills or communications skills? Identifying the needs of your students, yourself, and your program is the first exercise in successful business partner recruiting.

Use the chart below to help identify your needs:

		Attributes, Skills, Talents Required by a Partner	Prospective Candidates	Contact Information
A. Program Needs				
1	Funding	Tenacious, large number of contacts, has fundraising background or experience	Sylvia Jones – ABC Bank Foundation	sjones@abc.com 555-555-5555
2				
3				
4				
B. Student Needs				
1				
2				
3				
4				
C. Other Needs				
1				
2				
3				
4				

3.4 How to Connect to Prospective Partners

As noted in Section 3.2, you have much more access to prospective partners than you might think: By leveraging your personal or professional networks, you should have access to a long list of businesses in your field. But it's one thing to know you have access to them — how do you actually introduce yourself and guide them in to a partnership?

There are four critical components of your work to guide prospective partners into your program. These include:

◊   The introduction

◊   Learning about them

◊   Educating them

◊   Getting on the same team

We'll explore each of these in turn.

The Introduction

Once you have identified who you're going to contact, you need to proactively reach out to prospective partners. If you found out about your prospect through someone in your network, the best thing you can do is leverage that relationship as much as possible in making the introduction. Ideally, your contact will reach out to the business, introduce your program, and ask if they would be willing to have a phone call or meeting with you. Even better would be to have them join the call or meeting! This kind of introduction, facilitated by someone who they know and trust, is by far the best approach.

Since your contact identified the connection in the first place, he or she will likely have an idea of what they want to say to their associate. But if they would like some guidance, let them know that they might focus on the prospect's interest, and suggest you as a solution. For example:

> *"Hi Bob, this is John Smith. Listen, I know your company hires a fair number of welders, and that you've had trouble finding good people. I know the head of the welding program at [School Name], and I know that they're interested in building their program. I was wondering if I could ask him to give you a call to talk?"*

With this kind of introduction, your contact has given the business a powerful reason to want to talk to you; a first meeting is very likely at this point.

In some cases, your contact may not be able to personally make contact on your behalf, but permit you to use their name. (Always ask permission before using someone's name of course.) While a direct introduction is still ideal, being able to refer to a mutual contact is a close second.

If you have no personal connection to the business, it's still entirely possible to reach out on your own: Remember that, even though your prospect doesn't realize it yet, you have powerful shared interests, and you could both benefit greatly by working together. You're not asking for charity, and you're not selling anything: You're exploring a professional relationship of shared benefit.

When you make the introductory outreach yourself, with or without being able to reference a shared connection, there are a few ways you can go:

Letter

Many schools send out letters each year to hundreds of businesses, inviting them to join the school as a partner. These are usually form letters, and almost always fail to get a response. Letters — even personalized letters — require a fair amount of effort to respond to, unlike e-mail or a phone call. We do not recommend" sending letters if you're interested in getting a response.

E-mail

E-mail can be a very effective tool. The key is to understand what it's good for

E-mail Introduction - Sample

I. With Referral

SUBJECT: Referred by John Smith re: welding training
Dear x,

I run the welding program at [School Name]. As I was talking to John Smith the other day, he mentioned that you might be interested in the work we're doing to prepare students for the field. I'd appreciate a chance to talk with you; we rely strongly on industry feedback and I'd like to learn what you're looking for in welders.

Would you be interested in connecting by phone? When would be a convenient time for you to talk this week?

Sincerely,

II. Without Referral

SUBJECT: Guidance on welding instruction needed for [School Name]
Dear x,

I run the welding program at [School Name]. I was hoping for a chance to meet with you at some point: I understand that your company hires welders on occasion, and I'd like to learn what you're looking for in your new employees. We prepare students for this field, and we rely strongly on industry feedback to tailor our instruction.

Would you be interested in connecting by phone? When would be a convenient time for you to talk this week?

Sincerely,

---

and what it's not. Specifically, e-mail is very good at reaching someone with a short and targeted message in order to elicit a specific action — in this case, to very quickly let someone know that they may have an interest in what you're doing, and then asking to talk by phone or in person. See the e-mail messages on the previous page as an example.

E-mail cannot carry the weight of the entire partnership development process. Don't send a five-page e-mail with every detail on your program, and don't send 10 attachments with brochures or newsletters either. The vast majority of people won't read this much content. Instead, use e-mail as a way to knock on someone's door, and move the conversation to another forum as soon as possible.

If you send two or three e-mails and don't receive a response, don't give up: Some people may be more comfortable with other channels of communication. Look instead to the phone or a personal introduction as a way to connect.

Phone Call

If you're more comfortable on the phone than online, phone calls can also be an effective way of making first contact with a new partner. As with e-mails, make your phone call short and to the point: Immediately establish why this is of interest to them ("I understand you hire welders from time to time"); explain the purpose of your call ("I run the welding program at [School Name], and we look for industry input to tailor our efforts"); and present the desired action ("I was wondering if I could come by to see your operation sometime?"). Some people may want to talk more at that moment, and that's fine; but you should open with a focus on your desired next step in case they're busy.

Meeting at Industry Event

An unexpected face-to-face meeting (or expected, if you were angling for an introduction) is a bit of a different scenario. It's a more conversational setting: You'll have more time to talk about your work and establish that element of shared interest. But it does help to be prepared for these situations to make sure you get across your main points. For example, in these kinds of chance meetings, you might look for opportunities to mention:

◊ The number of students who go through your program each year; ideally, the number of students who enter the field

◊ Outside affirmation of your work — the fact that students earn industry credentials or get credits at a local college

◊ The fact that you're using current technology to prepare students for what they'll find in the workplace

◊ Members of your advisory board, or any current business partners, they might know

◊ Any students you know who are now working with your prospective partner's company

Industry meetings give you an opportunity to be much more conversational; just remember to turn the conversation back to your prospective partner, asking about their job, their company, and their background. If the conversation goes well, you'll find it very easy to ask for a follow-up meeting to talk further.

The First Meeting

If your introductory call or e-mail was successful, you've secured an opportunity to talk further with your future partner. If at all possible, try to meet with them in person rather than talking over the phone: A face-to-face meeting is much better for building relationships than a phone call.

Two considerations when setting up your first meeting:

◊   At this first meeting, make an effort to have one of your advocates at the table, such as the person who made the initial referral, someone from your advisory board, or one of your business partners. You want one of their professional peers there to explain firsthand why they're committed to your program. But if you can't secure that person for the initial meeting, you should still plan on meeting with your prospective partner as soon as you can (ideally within a week or two of the initial contact).

◊   Where should you meet? Before you enter a partnership, you'll want your business contact to visit your school. But for your first meeting, you should try to meet at their place of work. Since you initiated the relationship, you should make the time commitment to travel to their business; besides, it conveys the message that you want to learn more about what they do. And to that end, be sure to ask for a tour of their facility so you can see what they do firsthand — you'll get a chance to scope out their operation to identify possible work-based learning opportunities, and you may be introduced to others at the company.

At this first meeting, you'll want to focus on three objectives:

Learning about them

One of the most important things you can do at this meeting is ask questions and be sincerely interested in the answers. Your prospective partner will begin to understand that you care about their problems and challenges, which will go a long way towards establishing a shared approach. This kind of fact-finding will also provide the information you need to start scoping out the kind of partnership model that will make sense for you both.

Educating them

When you talk about your program, speak in terms that will be of interest to them, like how you're trying to prepare students for the realities of the workplace, and how you're emphasizing workplace skills as well as technical skills. Bring written materials on your program that they can take with them, and emphasize the impact of your work on students by bringing photos of students in action and talking about their accomplishments and future plans.

Talk in positive terms about all that you're achieving; don't emphasize the negative, or fixate on your needs and shortcomings. Remember that people want to be associated with a success not pulled into a rescue operation.

Getting on the same team

Emphasize your shared interests; try to establish a relationship where you're both on the same side, dealing with a common problem. Use "we" and "us" more than "you" or "me."

If all goes well, you will have each learned about the other's operations and found common ground for talking further about how you can work together. You may have even started to brainstorm specific partnership ideas. But to fully engage your prospective partner and give them the information they need to inform the planning process, it usually makes sense to bring them to your school so they can see your program for themselves.

If they're not interested in visiting your program right now, look for some other action step to keep the door open and gain some value from the connection. You might ask if there's someone else at the company you could talk to about specific, low-commitment opportunities ("We try to take students out on site visits — who could I talk to about setting that up?"). You might ask them to serve as an expert in some way ("Each year we survey employers on needed skill sets — can we include you in that survey?"). Or you might just look for a commitment to talk again when the timing might be better ("I understand this merger is preventing you from getting involved in anything right now. Can we touch base in six months to see where things stand?").

The Second Meeting

If your prospective partner is interested in visiting your program, try to make sure the meeting happens during the school day: You want them to have a chance to meet your students and see your teachers in action. Better yet, try to schedule the visit for a day when some of your business partners are on campus, which will reinforce the idea that businesses are active in your program.

As you tour the building, remember to highlight the successes and the positive aspects of your program: Don't focus on the shortcomings, the needs, or the resource challenges. And keep your focus on the students — too many educators (especially administrators) default to talking about the facilities.

Once you've talked and visited one anothers' sites, you'll likely have some idea as to how you can work together. They may fit in with one of your existing partnership models, perhaps taking a place on your advisory board, joining as a mentor or volunteer, or participating in some other existing initiative. If you and your partner are interested in developing a new program, the models outlined in Section 2 will provide some good guidance as to how to do that; once you have the parameters outlined, all that remains is to define the specifics and secure a commitment. The next two units will cover those steps.

3.5 Making the Pitch

As your relationship with your prospective partner has developed, you've had a chance to explore your respective needs and goals and the kinds of resources you can each bring to the table.

At some point you'll feel ready to go from general exploratory discussions to putting a concrete proposal on the table — a plan that defines specifically what the partnership looks like, what each of the stakeholders gets out of it, who's responsible for each piece, and how you'll know that it's working.

There's no single right way to do this. You and your partner may have sketched this out over time, as your relationship has progressed, or they may have been hesitant to suggest anything, expecting you to take the lead.

Whatever the case, when it's time to put a proposal on the table, you'll want to make sure it includes the following elements:

◊ **Partnership Description** – In concrete terms, you'll want to lay out what the partnership looks like: If it's a career mentoring program, for example, you'll want to define how many times per month students meet with their mentors and for how long, how many students and adults will participate, who will oversee the program, and what the career areas are that they will explore.

◊ **Stakeholder Roles** – You should identify each of the stakeholders, including students, your partner, your school, and anyone else with a role to play (administrators, parents, etc.) and figure out what that role is.

◊ **Targeted Outcomes** – Knowing who will be involved in the program, you should set clearly defined outcomes for each stakeholder, so you can make it clear what they'll get in return for their participation.

◊ **Measurement** – For each of the key stakeholder outcomes, you should decide how you'll measure impact. These could be qualitative measures like increased student understanding of certain careers, or they could be quantitative, like boosting graduation rates among participating students by 10 percent.

◊ **Partner Responsibilities** – You should be very explicit in listing out the responsibilities of each partner. Who will recruit the mentors, and who will recruit the students? Who's responsible for the background checks on the mentors? Who will host the meetings? Who sets up site visits and handles transportation? Who will manage the measurement function?

Sometimes this can be handled through a simple conversation, particularly when you've already discussed some of the details in general terms. It might be sufficient to work through the elements face to face, doing no more than jotting down the details in a notepad so you have a written record of the conversation. Other times, particularly for larger partnership proposals or for partners who need to get approval from other parties, you'll want to prepare a more formal proposal outlining the partnership idea you discussed.

Writing Winning Partnership Proposals

In partnership development, sometimes a strong proposal can make all the difference in getting your prospective partner to commit. Proposals are certainly not required in every situation: smaller-scale initiatives rarely justify them, and they are not always needed when talking with a sole decision-maker. But in cases where you're requesting a large commitment, or when many people are involved in the decision to partner with you, a well-written proposal is an indispensable tool in securing an agreement.

It is important to note that writing and submitting a proposal should be the last step, not the first, in the partnership development process. A proposal should only be developed after developing a relationship and talking at length about what you each want to accomplish (for the partners and for the students), how you want to measure those accomplishments, and what each party is able to bring to the table.

This information is critical in creating a customized partnership plan that provides a return to your partners as they define it, and it allows you to frame your proposed partnership in terms that your partner will see as relevant to his or her business or organization.

Elements of a Successful Proposal

The exact structure of your proposals will vary based on your audience and what you're trying to do. But the elements below should be addressed in some way:

<u>**Goals/Benefits**</u>
At an early point in the proposal — preferably on the first page — clearly lay out the benefits of the partnership in terms of both student/school outcomes and partner outcomes. Sample text:

> *"By working together, [partner] and [school] have an opportunity to increase interest in science, and therefore impact career awareness and selection, among [targeted student population]. By working with [school] on this initiative and promoting its successes, [partner] will not only be able to present itself as a socially committed company among its customers and stakeholders, but will also realize specific benefits including increased employee morale and an improved labor pool as these students enter the workforce."*

Remember that the benefits highlighted here must be identified on the basis of your partner's interests and backed up by specifics later in the proposal. Don't promise higher morale, for example, if there's no way to develop and measure it.

Key Project Participants

It's helpful to list the key players in the partnership so that your new partner knows who is involved, what their role is, and whether they've already committed to the project. Be sure to include your school or district on the list and identify their contribution (such as a commitment of staff time, facilities, or access to data).

Analysis of Current Situation

This section combines a description of where things currently stand with a statement of need — in other words, why the current state is unsatisfactory. As an example, you could explain that graduation rates for your targeted student population are 20 percent below those of other groups, and outline the implications of that in terms of poverty rates and a shortage in the local workforce. This will set up the need for your proposed solution.

Proposed Solution

This is the "meat" of the proposal: a description of how your program will help students get from point A to point B. You should be sure to highlight the evidence backing up your proposed solution: You don't need to write a dissertation by any means, but your partners must feel confident that your solution is backed by evidence and has a reasonable chance of success.

Measurement/Evaluation

If someone is going to invest their time, talents, and treasure in your partnership initiative, they need to have a reasonable expectation that their investment is going to produce results. Once you've laid out your solution, you must explain how you'll measure success according to your objectives. This could be by tracking test scores, but it could also involve pre-/post-assessments of interest, graduation rates, or the percentage of students exploring postsecondary opportunities. Include interim measures (to guide the development of the program) as well as final outcome measures. The key is to find measurements that are tied to your objectives and that your partners find to be relevant.

Remember also to measure the returns desired by your partner, whether those relate to career awareness, workforce preparation, employee morale, community goodwill, or some other goal. These measures, and responsibility for tracking them, may come from your partner — but they should be referenced so it's clear that they are being included in the plan.

What Your Partner Will Provide

The point of a proposal is to secure a commitment from your prospective partner; you must therefore spell out exactly what you're asking of them. Be as specific as possible: Instead of asking for volunteers, ask for five volunteers to be present at the school from 3 to 4:30pm on Mondays and Thursdays in October. And ask them to participate in a review or advisory board as well; they will want ongoing input into your work.

What Your Partner Will Receive

In the beginning of the proposal, you offered general information on the benefits your partner will receive; you should provide specifics on those benefits in the body of the document. This includes describing how those benefits will be defined and measured, in terms relevant to your partner. For example, you may say that "by allowing employees to participate as mentors, [partner] can expect to see an improvement in employee morale. [Partner] can track this through its annual employee survey or by having employees participate in a pre-/post-survey."

Signature Lines

A proposal is a request for a commitment; get yours in writing by asking an authorized representative of your partner to sign the agreement. Have the proper person within your organization sign it as well. A signed proposal is a valuable resource because it can help clear up any confusion over either party's role and can help keep the terms of the relationship in place in the event of a leadership change.

About Your Organization

It will be helpful to provide information about your school, district, or nonprofit organization as an appendix to your proposal. Remember that some of the people reading the proposal may not have been involved in discussions. In addition to sharing basic facts, you might present yourself as an attractive partner by highlighting areas of strength and recent accomplishments; you can also significantly strengthen your case by outlining other past or current partnership successes.

The key with any successful proposal is to speak from the point of view of your prospective partner. If you can explain in ways that are personally meaningful to them what they will get in exchange for their participation (i.e., their ROI), your proposals will be well received and it will be much more likely that those prospective partners will join with you as a powerful ally in your work to improve student outcomes.

Once You've Made the Pitch

Your proposal, whether verbal or written, isn't a "take it or leave it" deal. Your partner may want to make some changes (which is a good sign, since it means they're likely on board with some tweaks). They'll probably have some questions as well — these questions may be easy to answer or may expose some holes in your plan. Again, this is a good sign, as it means your pitch is being taken seriously.

All of the work you've done should result in a "sale." But in order to "seal the deal," you sometimes have to ask the question directly:

◊   "Are you ready to join our advisory board?"

◊   "So, can I count on you for this career mentoring program?"

◊   "Can we agree that you'll make a contribution of $_____?"

◊   "When can you give a firm commitment to this project?"

All of these questions are "closing questions" that can be answered with a "Yes" or "No." If the answer is "Yes," then you've accomplished your goal. If the answer is "No" or "Not yet," then the prospect still has some questions in his/her mind. You might then say,

◊   "What other information can I share with you to help your decision?"

◊   "Is there something I haven't fully explained?"

◊   "Is there a reason or concern you have that I haven't fully addressed?"

Hopefully, open-ended questions like these will uncover something that you can address and allow you to then try a "closing question" again.

Famed salesperson Zig Ziglar said that "People don't change their minds. But sometimes they make new decisions based on new information." If you get a "no," try to ascertain the real reason — time availability, personality conflict with someone else on the project, or perhaps a lack of support from the individual's manager. If any of these issues change, your prospective partner could make a "yes" decision sometime in the future.

Assuming your partner is ready to move ahead, there's just one more step: Sealing the deal, or setting up a formal agreement and putting some things in place to maximize your chances for success!

3.6 Sealing the Deal

Congratulations! Your prospective partner is now an actual partner: They've agreed to the partnership you proposed and are ready to start working. There are just a few things you need to do in order to get things off on the right foot:

◊ **Get commitments in writing.** Spell out each party's responsibilities and get each party to sign off. (See the sample below.)

◊ **Start to build other relationships in the organization.** One reason that partnerships fail is turnover: When one of the program leaders leaves their organization, it's easy for the project to die for lack of any other internal support. Find that support before it's needed.

◊ **Get some early "wins."** Set some early goals and meet them to give the project some momentum. They can be small — but early successes will build trust between the partners and a positive feeling about the work.

◊ **Spread the good word!** Let people inside each of your organizations know about the new partnership. This is the first step to building internal support and finding participants once you get started.

Partnership Agreement - Sample

This document outlines the responsibilities of [School Name] and [Business Name] as they establish a partnership to help students explore career opportunities and workplace realities in the welding profession.

For the 2014–2015 school year, [School Name] agrees to the following:

- Recruit no more than 20 students for the program
- Secure parent signatures on permission slips
- Administer background checks on adult volunteers
- Provide transportation up to once per month to [Business Name] for site visits
- Administer pre- and post-surveys to students over the course of the program to gauge the impact on their career plans and knowledge of the field

For the 2014–2015 school year, [Business Name] agrees to the following:

- Recruit 20 employees to mentor participating students
- Allow those employees to spend up to two hours per month with students "on the clock" and agree that employees will not be penalized for any lost production during that time
- Train students on safety procedures before allowing them into the work area; provide safety equipment as needed
- Make a donation of $500 for classroom materials related to this program
- Administer pre- and post-surveys to participating employees over the course of the program to get feedback on the program and gauge any change in employee motivation or morale

With their signatures below, both parties the responsibilities listed above.

[School Name Signature]   [Business Name Signature]

Section IV

Measuring Partnership Outcomes

EET

4.1 Why Evaluate?

It's easy to understand why some people might skip over evaluation when planning their partnerships. It comes down to a lack of resources: They don't have the time, money, or expertise to do it. Many partnership leaders have made the argument that "every dollar we put into evaluation is a dollar we're not spending on the kids."

While it is technically true that money spent on evaluation cannot be spent elsewhere, the benefits of evaluating your work far outweigh the costs. In fact, if you're able to produce hard data that proves the value of your work, you will likely be able to attract far more support for your program than you ever could have without that data. Importantly, it will also help you build a case to school and district leaders for the continued funding of your program, since many CTE or advanced STEM programs are treated as electives.

There are actually several benefits of evaluating your partnerships:

Ensuring your program is achieving results for students
Too many programs fail to evaluate, assuming that their programs are designed well and that their hard work is having a positive impact. But that's not always the case. Regardless of your intention, your program may not be producing any positive outcomes, or it may be producing different outcomes than you planned for. The experiences of DARE (in the box below) are a good example of this.

Securing ongoing support from partner districts
While your district may not be providing direct funding for supplemental partnership programs, it is likely contributing in ways such as offering free space for meetings, handling program administration (background checks, parent permission slips), covering the cost of staff time, and supporting your work in other ways. If you want to continue benefiting from district support, make sure it sees the payoff.

The Value of Evaluation — The DARE Program

We often assume that if we design an education program well and work hard at it it will produce the outcomes we want. As DARE proved, that's not always the case.

The DARE program (Drug Abuse Resistance Education) was created to prevent the use of controlled drugs, membership in gangs, and violent behavior. And the design of this awareness and prevention program made sense: Develop a curriculum, train local police officers to deliver it, and send them out to schools to talk with children about the dangers of drugs and illicit lifestyles. And since 1988, these officers have reached millions of students, assuming they were making an impact on these issues.

But as independent evaluations of the program began to be published, each one found either that the program had no long-term effect or that it even contributed to increased experimentation in students' later years.

As a result of this data, DARE completely revamped its program, adopting an evidence-based program from Penn State University that was listed on the National Registry of Evidence-based Programs and Practices (NREPP).

In this case, evaluation showed that common sense doesn't always produce results — and the work of the DARE program will have a far greater impact as a result.

Securing/expanding support from businesses

Businesses, foundations, and increasingly even school districts think in terms of return on investment, or ROI. To attract and sustain supporters, you'll need to show them in measurable terms what impact you're having: That's the only way for your business partners to gauge whether their investment in your partnership was worthwhile and whether it should continue.

In addition to serving the interests of your current partner, a "measurement mentality" will help you attract new partners. In a 2007 survey of business coalition leaders, participants were asked what factors they consider when choosing education partners. An interest in measurable outcomes was the second most important criterion, as shown in the following table:

Survey Item	%
What criteria do you use when selecting partners?	
Willingness to collaborate	84.7%
Interest in measurable outcomes	67.6%
Commitment to the project	64.0%
Needs of the student body	48.6%
Existing relationship with coalition	33.3%
Accessibility to location	21.6%
Other	18.0%

Source: Coalition Leaders Speak Out on Education, DeHavilland Associates, 2007

Finding ways to improve your impact

Once you start tracking your outcomes, you'll be able to start benchmarking: In other words, since you know what outcomes you're producing now, you'll be able to tweak your model to see whether you can have an even greater impact.

Finding unexpected areas of impact

A thorough evaluation will look at multiple types of potential impact; you may learn that you're having an effect in areas you hadn't even considered, such as boosting self-efficacy or self-image.

Increasing the importance of partnerships in schools and communities

If you prove that you can take limited resources and produce real and measurable outcomes for students, especially in a time of limited resources and increased demands, you will raise the profile of partnerships with school and district leaders, the business community, parents, and other stakeholders. This can encourage both internal and external stakeholders to make these kinds of relationships a greater priority going forward.

As you can see, there are several very good reasons to evaluate your partnership program(s). But how do you do it?

4.2 The Logic Model

Note: The approach to Logic Models outlined in this section has been simplified and adapted to the particular needs of business/education partnerships. For a comprehensive review of Logic Models and their use in evaluation, start with the resources available from the Program Development & Evaluation website of the University of Wisconsin Extension: www.uwex.edu/ces/pdande/index.html.

Partnership design and evaluation can be intimidating: How do you design a program that works? How do you know what to measure, and how? The best place to start is building a Logic Model for your partnership.

Basic Elements of a Logic Model

As you might guess, a Logic Model lays out the thinking behind your partnership program. It addresses your starting point, your desired end point, and what has to happen in between to create the change you want, commonly referred to as your intervention. The basic model is this:

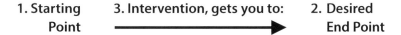

1. Starting Point   3. Intervention, gets you to: 2. Desired End Point

Notice that the items above are numbered out of order: That's because you need to figure out what success looks like before you can decide on the kind of intervention you need to achieve it.

The best way to start is by reviewing the desired ROI you set for each of the primary stakeholders at the beginning of your partnership planning process. If your business partner's ROI was a better pipeline of qualified workers, for example, how can you define that? Do they want to measure the total number of applicants? The total number of employees they hire each year directly from your school? The total number of applicants with a specific certification? Figure out exactly what that ROI means to them, in concrete terms, and then work through that same process for each of the ROI statements for your business partner, your school, and your students. (The next section, Types of Outcomes, will look more closely at this issue.)

Once you know the kinds of things you'll be tracking, you'll need to do two things before you can go much farther:

◊ **Get a baseline reading** – If you want to go from point A to point B, you need to know what point A looks like. If you want to increase the graduation rate by 20 percent, what is the graduation rate now? If you want to boost the number of qualified applicants by 30 percent, what are the current numbers?

◊ **Agree on a finish line** – Since you're building a partnership of equals, all of the partners have to agree on how success will be measured. Granted, certain partners will have more of a voice in their core areas; your business partner will be in a better position to determine a reasonable increase in employee morale, and you'll be in a better position to decide on a goal for graduation rates. But taken as a whole, all of the partners must sign off on the goals of the partnership. This will have some positive side effects, such as having everyone talk in terms of measurable goals, and avoiding any conflicts at the end of the program regarding what the program was intended to achieve.

When it comes to program outcomes, be aware that some partnerships may decide to break these into short-term, medium-term, and long-term elements, and that you might find it helpful to do that as well. For the purposes of this section, we'll simply group them together.

The Intervention

If you're trying to move from point A to point B, your intervention is your vehicle for getting there. There are three elements of the intervention that need to be accounted for in your Logic Model:

◊ **Resources** – Every program requires resources, whether those are financial donations, in-kind goods and services, volunteer and staff time, free space for meetings, or other kinds of support. Resources fuel your partnership the way oxygen fuels a fire: The more you supply, the bigger the fire and the brighter the flame. Make sure that the level of resources you have is proportionate to the size of the impact you want to make, and either increase your resources or reduce your expectations as needed.

◊ **Activities** – Activities are the actual action steps you take as part of your partnership program. These should be designed with your goal in mind; for every activity you include in your plan, you should have a clear understanding as to how that is going to help you reach your goal. That's not to say that every single activity has to feed directly to the primary goal: You may decide that a year-end celebration is a good reinforcing tool and that your students and volunteers will want to be recognized. But you should know why you're doing things in order to keep a focus on your targets.

◊ **Participants** – For each of your activities, you'll want to know who's involved and who's responsible. Planning out your roles in this way allows you to set expectations and clearly define the roles of the partners. It also helps you identify the resources you'll need to have in place (such as volunteers, or funding for staff members) in order to run a successful program.

The sample Logic Model chart on the opposite page lays out a possible model for a career exploration and mentoring program between a school and a local

Logic Model - Sample Chart

This chart outlines a Logic Model for a career exploration and mentoring program. A blank chart is found on the next page for use in laying out your own programs.

Starting Point	+	Resources	+	Activities	+	Participants	=	End Point

Students

This program serves 11th and 12th grade CTE students who may be interested in the manufacturing field.

- Currently have an 80 percent graduation rate
- 60 percent of graduates go for postsecondary education
- Estimated 25 percent of all students go into manufacturing
- ABC Manufacturing hires 10 students per year (some after college)

ABC Manufacturing

ABC is facing challenges finding qualified workers, and wants to give employees opportunities to share their knowledge and enthusiasm.

- ABC Manufacturing hires 10 of our students per year (some after college)
- Only one-third of the applicants from our school were hired (30 applicants total)
- Employees asking for volunteer opportunities

School

- Recruit students
- Handle paperwork (background checks, permission slips)
- Space for on-campus meetings
- Transportation to ABC facility
- Track student data with help of part-time admin support

ABC Manufacturing

- Recruit volunteers and mentors
- Train employees on working with students
- Give employees paid time off to participate in program
- Contribute $1,000 to cover cost of part-time admin for data gathering

Career Exploration

- ABC employees speak to students five times per year about their jobs and their career paths
- ABC employees host a booth at career fair
- All CTE students visit ABC for a site tour

Career Mentoring

- 20 ABC employees interviewed and selected for mentoring program
- ABC employees meet with mentees once per month at school and work sites to introduce them to career options and help them explore postsecondary and certification options

Career Exploration

- 10 ABC employees
- All CTE students (11th and 12th grade)
- Partnership administrator to coordinate meetings

Career Mentoring

- 20 ABC employees
- 20 students
- Partnership administrator to coordinate meetings

Student Goals

- CTE student graduation rate to 85 percent
- 70 percent of graduates go for postsecondary education
- Estimated 35 percent of all students go into manufacturing
- ABC manufacturing hires 15 students next year, 20 the second year, 25 the third year

ABC Goals

- Increase hiring to 15 next year, 20 the second year, 25 the third year
- Increase employee satisfaction with volunteer opportunities (as noted on annual employee survey)

manufacturer. It specifies the starting points of the students and the business (this model did not have specified outcomes for school or staff), the resources that would fuel the program, the activities that would be completed (including administrative tasks like background checks), who was responsible for each task, and specific, measurable outcomes broken out by stakeholder, and mirroring the categories used in the beginning.

As you develop your own Logic Models, you can modify the chart as you see fit. You may decide to break out the short-term, medium-term, and long-term outcomes of your partnership; you may decide to draw arrows between specific activities and specific end goals. The idea is to use this in a way that makes sense to you and that allows you to see the connections between where you're starting, what you're doing, and what you're accomplishing.

Once you've completed one of these charts, it can be helpful to step back and ask yourself: Is this reasonable? Are these resources and activities really enough to produce these end goals? Am I sure that these activities are effective methods of creating the change that I want? Are these participants going to be available for this project, are they reliable, and are they capable of managing the pieces that I've assigned to them?

Hopefully you'll find that thinking through the Logic Model not only helps you in your evaluation efforts, but also provides a useful check on your entire approach to your partnership. By including your partner in this process, you'll likely also find that their engagement and commitment to the partnership will become more grounded as well.

EET: Logic Model for Partnerships

Fill out the chart below as you develop your partnership model.

Starting Point				End Point
Resources +	Activities +	Participants =		

4.3 Outcomes and Measurement Tools

For any partnership, there are usually a lot of different ways to measure student (and partner) outcomes, and there's usually no one right way of doing it. For a career exploration program, for example, do you base your evaluation on measuring how much time students spend watching career videos? How they score on a quiz about careers? Student questionnaires on their level of interest? Teachers' evaluations of students' level of interest? A long-term study showing the courses that students end up taking, or the careers they enter? None of these are automatically right or wrong; it's up to you and your partners to decide which metrics really capture what you're trying to measure.

As you start to think about defining and measuring outcomes, it's important to realize that there are two types of information that you can collect:

◊ **Qualitative measures** – It helps to think about qualitative data as "words" as opposed to "numbers." Qualitative data comprise a softer, more exploratory set of information. While they don't offer the hard proof available from quantitative data, they do allow you to get a more personal feel for what's happening and give you the flexibility to explore a topic more deeply. Qualitative research is used to get information on "hard to measure" items and is also often used earlier in a project, when you're still trying to define your program. Common data collection methods used in qualitative research are focus groups, interviews, and observations.

◊ **Quantitative measures** --You can think of quantitative data as "numbers" rather than "words." These data include more definitive, factual information, usually represented through numbers or percentages, such as the number of students hired by a company, graduation rates, attendance figures, test scores, or survey results.

There is a place for both qualitative and quantitative measurement in your program; it really depends what you're trying to accomplish and the most appropriate model for measuring outcomes as you've defined them. But don't try to evaluate your program solely on qualitative measures. It's fine to share the impressions of program leaders on how students are responding to a program, but if you don't couple that with some harder measures of student progress, you run the risk of being labeled another "feel-good" program and losing the support of your partners.

With that in mind, this chapter presents a number of outcomes that you can consider as you work to define your terms, along with some ways of measuring each outcome. This is in no way a complete list but rather more of an idea-starter to help you think about ways of setting your own measurements. You can choose or modify any or all of these as it makes sense in your unique situation.

Student Outcomes

School-based statistics

Schools collect and report data on several fronts; if it's appropriate to your program, you can track students' individual performance on these same values and report on their progress. This approach has some advantages: It will be easily understood by your partners and the public, for example; you'll be able to compare your students' performance against the entire school; and the school or district might be able to use student IDs to pull their numbers without your having to do the tracking yourself. (Of course, student data privacy laws may need to be accommodated.)

Some of the more common data points that schools record:

◊ Graduation rates

◊ Attendance rates

◊ Incidence rates

◊ Scores on state assessments, including technical skill assessments

◊ Other official assessments (WorkKeys, PSAT, SAT, ACT, etc.)

◊ Student grades

These are all quantitative values that can likely be gathered through existing channels, making them attractive as part of your evaluation mix.

Employability skills

Many employers say finding employees with employability skills ("soft skills") is a greater issue than finding workers with needed technical skills. You may decide to identify a specific set of employability skills and find ways to measure them, perhaps through a student self-assessment, by having a work-based learning coordinator or company employees evaluate an intern using your questionnaire or using employability skills assessments offered by NOCTI, CTECS, or others.

Industry certifications

Attainment of industry certifications is a widely recognized point of achievement that can be easily tracked by partners. Note that since most schools do not pay for certification tests, those schools are generally not able to access scores and achievement levels; data will need to come from students or their sponsors.

Work experience

You might decide that gaining a certain level of work experience, through part-time jobs, internships, or apprenticeships, is an important benchmark for your program; this could be particularly important in an employment preparation program, for example. Assessment can be as simple as tracking employment hours, though you may consider adding secondary measures like student self-assessments or employer assessments to gauge the quality of the experience.

Participation in extracurricular activities

Extracurricular activities are an important indicator of interest, and can provide many competitive or leadership opportunities. Track students' out-of-school efforts to see what organizations they join, whether they're active, whether they take a leadership role, and whether they participate in local, state, or national competitions.

Course selection

If you want to explore a students' level of engagement or interest in a career or academic field, consider tracking the courses they select over time. Selecting a concentration of courses in a certain area, or aiming for the most challenging level of instruction, is an indication of interest.

Completion Rate for Program Sequence

One indicator of a high quality CTE or STEM program is the percentage of program participants who progress from one course to the next, ultimately then completing the program sequence. While not every student will complete the sequence due to changed interests or scheduling challenges, a significant number should be vested in the program so that they complete the highest possible level.

Postsecondary plans

If you're interested in looking at students' dedication to a career path and/or their commitment to pursuing postsecondary education, there are a number of metrics that indicate their preparedness and their plans:

◊ Track the number of college credits they pursue while still in high school.

◊ Track participation in college and career fairs and whether they have talked with previous employers, military representatives, or others about their future.

◊ Find out if they have explored financial aid options, including completion of a FAFSA (Free Application for Federal Student Aid) form.

◊ Develop a student survey to gauge their knowledge of, and interest in, selected postsecondary options.

◊ Assess their academic preparedness for college-level work using some of the school-based indicators mentioned on the previous page.

Business Partner Outcomes

Your business partners will obviously take the lead on deciding exactly how to define their desired outcomes and how they should be measured. But schools should take an active role as supportive partners, given that they'll participate in defining the structure of the partnership and likely in collecting some of the data. Some possible outcomes in which your partner may be interested:

Hiring new employees

One of the main reasons businesses partner with CTE programs is to identify, prepare, and hire new employees; therefore, this will probably be one of the first things your partners will want to track. Find out how they track this information (do they log all resumes or job inquiries? Do they only track this information from interviews, or from hires?) and ask if there are ways in which you can supplement their efforts, such as asking students about their interests in local employers or about which employers they have applied to.

Quality/size of the labor pool

In addition to their own hiring reviews, your partner may keep tabs on the quality and size of the local labor pool in certain fields. In this case, they may care as much about students' awareness of opportunities in certain industries or professions as they care about technical skills. Student surveys would be a good fit for this analysis, or your partner may track the volume of applications they receive for posted jobs.

Employee morale

There are many documented benefits for employees who volunteer or mentor students, one of the greatest being an increase in employee morale. If your business partner does any sort of regular employee surveys, he or she can add a question asking whether the employee has participated in your program and then see whether those employees have a higher level of workplace satisfaction than those who did not participate.

Employee retention

Another benefit employers receive from social partnerships is that participating employees tend to stay with a company longer than nonparticipating employees. Your business partner should be able to determine whether employee retention is influenced by participation in your partnership.

Employee skill development

In some partnership models, such as those where your partner serves on advisory boards or lends professional expertise to your school, your partners' employees may have an opportunity to develop new technical or leadership skills. Management should be able to keep tabs on the impact of their involvement in your work to see whether those new skills are similarly benefiting their company.

Company brand/awareness among stakeholders or the community

If public visibility is important to your partner, whether among specific groups (like customers, vendors, unions, or regulators) or among the community overall, they'll want to track awareness of the company's good work. In cases like these, your program will probably have some type of public outreach element, such as your partner including mentions of your program in their newsletter or other public communications, and they'll likely have the tools needed to gauge changes in public awareness and perceptions.

School/Educator Outcomes

Partnerships are first and foremost about improving students' lives. But outcomes for schools, and for educators in particular, are important as well. Historically, partnerships have been a "nice to have, not have to have" activity because of competing priorities and lack of a compelling ROI for the educators who have to make a large commitment to running such partnerships; focusing on returns specifically for that group will help to justify the partnership and provide greater rewards for those who make the partnerships possible.

Teacher quality

There are many approaches, both official and unofficial, to measuring teacher quality. It would be difficult, for example, to track the value of partnerships through a state's formal value-added assessment program, but other metrics, such as certifications earned by teachers, an interest in pursuing additional education, or personnel reviews by principals could help to gauge the impact of partnerships on participating teachers.

Resources

Partnerships do bring resources into a school, whether those are donations (money, equipment, classroom materials) or in-kind contributions. Many schools have a way of tracking donations like money, but not all are set up to log in-kind support.

Volunteer Hours

Volunteer hours are a particularly important type of community-provided resource: They reflect a real value provided to students and staff, and also serve as a measure of the community's commitment for your program. In addition, if you're applying for grants that require support from other sources, the value of volunteer hours often counts as a donation for that purpose. The Independent Sector website offers a commonly-accepted hourly rate for volunteer hours; see http://independentsector.org/volunteer_time for the current hourly rate.

Community support

It can be hard to get an accurate gauge of community support; even if your district does annual surveys of community or parent satisfaction, it would be hard to isolate the impact of your partnership on the overall result. But there are alternative approaches: You can collect letters of appreciation from parents and students, ask partners for testimonials, and collect press clippings detailing the work of your partnership.

Teacher/administration morale and retention

It might be hard to collect hard data on the impact of your partnership on teacher morale; even if your school or state conducts an annual survey of teachers on working conditions, it would be difficult to isolate the impact of your partnership. In a case like this, interviews with participating teachers may be the best approach to finding out what kind of difference your program has made in their lives. You might consider asking educators for testimonials that you can share with others.

Program performance

As your partnerships grow in size and number, their impact will likely show up in the way your program is viewed by others. Your graduation rates may improve; students may be more likely to find work in your field; you may have a case full of trophies from various competitions. All of these speak to the quality of your program, and of your partnerships.

Partnership Outcomes

If your program is large enough, you might want to find ways of evaluating the performance of the program itself. This will allow you to make sure it's being managed well, run effectively, and providing a rewarding experience for your stakeholders.

Financial Performance

Some programs, particularly those that require significant resources or those operating at a large scale, should look at resource management to see whether the program is being run efficiently and cost-effectively. If you invest in recruiting students (publishing ads, distributing flyers, advertising online), you should be able to calculate the response rate you get to various marketing efforts and how much it costs you to attract each participant. You might also want to review cash flow management to see how quickly resources come in versus how quickly they go out (your "burn rate") and calculate how much of a financial cushion your program needs to avoid shortfalls that could disrupt your program.

Management

You might want to look at the "people" side of your program to make sure it's being managed well and that stakeholders are walking away with a positive experience (in addition to concrete positive outcomes):

◊ **Retention rate** – If 50 students sign on at the program launch, how many are left by the time you're done? If you're losing a lot of students along the way, there could be issues with the way the program is being presented to them or the way it's being run. You might also look at the retention of volunteers and partners.

◊ **Staff** – The teachers and volunteers who run your partnership activities on a day-to-day basis are a good source of independent feedback on your work. What's working and what's not? Are any elements confusing to, or disliked by, students or staff? How could the partnership operate more effectively in the future?

◊ **Communications** – Communications, particularly for a volunteer-driven partnership, can be challenging. Using both self-assessments and interviews or surveys, look back to see how well you've communicated with stakeholders. Can communications be improved going forward?

◊ **Operations** – Partnerships can involve lots of moving parts; it makes sense to review operations to see where the challenges lie and how they can be addressed in future years. Suppose your program involves transporting students to area businesses, and either your driver or your transportation turns out to be unreliable: This is the sort of issue that can harm your program but should be easy to identify and fix if you ask the right questions.

While this is by no means an exhaustive list of the ways in which you can assess your program's impact and quality, hopefully it will serve as a good starting point as you establish a set of metrics uniquely suited to your goals.

Partnership Planning Workshee Measurement and Evaluation

Once you've decided on your program goals, you can go through this worksheet with your business partners to decide on the specific outcomes you want to target for each stakeholder and how you'll measure them.

Targeted Student Outcomes   **Measured By:**

_____   _____

_____   _____

_____   _____

_____

Targeted Business Outcomes   **Measured By:**

_____   _____

_____   _____

_____   _____

_____

Targeted School/Admin Outcomes   **Measured By:**

_____   _____

_____   _____

_____   _____

_____

4.4 Tips, Tricks, and Effective Practices

There's more to evaluation than just deciding what type of data to collect and acquiring them. The evaluation function has to account for outside influences and circumstances, many of which can affect the quality of your analysis if they're not accounted for. In order to make sure you run an effective evaluation, you might consider some of the following ideas.

For All Partnerships

Don't overreach
It's great to be ambitious. But if you set your goals too high — if you suggest that your partnership is going to solve all your partners' hiring issues, or that it will double their company's stock price — you'll look unrealistic and inevitably fall short, casting doubt about the value of your program. It's better to be realistic about what your partnership will achieve given the resources you have available and the scope of the work being done.

Get a baseline
Remember that your evaluation is charting your progress in moving from point A to point B along some axis. Remember to get good data on your starting point before you begin your intervention — otherwise you won't have anything to compare your results against!

Be consistent with your surveys
If you're going to use surveys to capture information about people's knowledge and attitudes, use the exact same survey instrument both before and after your intervention. If you change the survey instrument, either mixing up or rewording the questions, or even just changing the order of the items, you're introducing a new variable into the process that doesn't need to be there. Be consistent and use the same survey materials at each point in the data collection process.

Train your people
If you have staff or volunteers assisting in data collection, make sure they understand why you're doing these surveys, why it's so important to your partnership, and how to do it correctly. If they don't know why they're doing all this extra work, they may not be motivated to do as thorough of a job as you need them to do.

Review and modify the program
Don't just collect and report your data: Use it to improve your program in future years. Did your program succeed in most areas but fall short in one or two? Look closely at the data from those elements, and if need be, go back to your students and volunteers to ask questions about what happened. You may find that your partnership effort didn't really lend itself to those outcomes, which leaves you

with a choice of either making big changes or removing that expectation. Or you may find that small changes in the program design can help you reach that goal after all.

For Large-Scale Partnerships

Independent evaluation

Most partnership programs operate at a small scale, and given limited resources, the program designers often double as the evaluators. But in an ideal world, evaluation is handled by an independent third party, such as a consultant or a university. This removes conflicts of interests, provides greater weight to the value of the evaluation, and usually results in a more thorough, higher-quality analysis. If the scale of your partnership program warrants it, consider looking for an independent third party to handle evaluation for you.

Random assignment

The gold standard in evaluation involves random assignment of participants: If 100 students apply to participate in the program, half of those are chosen through some randomized selection process, and both groups are tracked to see the differences in outcomes. This is rarely feasible in a local partnership-driven program because these programs are often too small to warrant this level of effort. But if you're interested in proving a certain model, or operating at a scale that warrants it, consider using some kind of random assignment mechanism so you can compare identical groups of students whose only difference is participation in your program.

Test/control model

Imagine for a moment that you hosted a career exploration program and found that the graduation rate for students in the program had increased by 10 percent. You would be pretty excited — at least until you found that some other initiative, maybe a new freshman experience or a new life skills program, boosted the graduation rate of the overall student body by 20 percent!

It's dangerous to look at your program's outcomes in a vacuum: There are other changes happening in your school that have no connection to your program, but that are influencing outcomes for students.

The best way to deal with this issue is to set up a test/control model: Gather data on your students (your "test" group), but also obtain comparable data for a different group of students at your school or district (your "control" group). That way you'll be able to see whether your students have improved thanks to your program or whether some outside factor changed outcomes for all students independent of your work.

4.5 Sharing Your Results

If your program is producing good outcomes, you should share that news! Not only will you be recognizing the hard work of your partners, volunteers, and students, but you'll also be paving the way for new partnerships in the future.

◊ Publish some sort of project summary that provides a description of your project, including who was involved and what happened, and present your data to highlight your outcomes.

◊ Make sure the right audiences see your results: Everyone wants to be part of something successful, and your project summary will let them know that you're producing positive outcomes for students and partners alike. Remember to reach out to the following audiences with your data:

» Current partners and other project participants

» Administrators and school board members

» Local businesses and connector organizations you'd like to work with in the future

» Postsecondary institutions in your area, including those you already work with and those with whom you'd like to develop a relationship

» Media outlets – newspapers, magazines, radio, and television

◊ Share your data through internal channels. Ask the school or district to publish it in its parent newsletter; post information on your website or print flyers to hand out to visitors and to send home to parents.

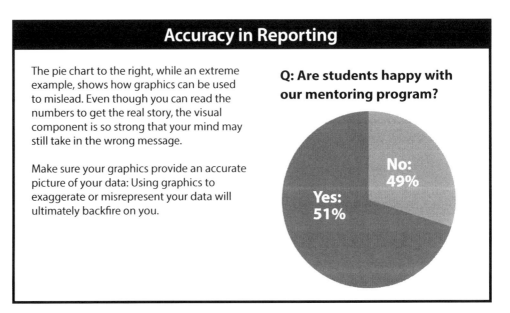

Accuracy in Reporting

The pie chart to the right, while an extreme example, shows how graphics can be used to mislead. Even though you can read the numbers to get the real story, the visual component is so strong that your mind may still take in the wrong message.

Make sure your graphics provide an accurate picture of your data: Using graphics to exaggerate or misrepresent your data will ultimately backfire on you.

Q: Are students happy with our mentoring program?

No: 49%

Yes: 51%

It's great to share positive outcomes from your program and your partnerships. But what should you do when your efforts don't produce any results?

◊ Use the information to inform your work – If your program didn't produce the outcomes you expected, find out why not. Was your plan based on other successful programs, and if so, did you deviate from their model in some way? Did anything happen during the course of your program to take you off track? Do think the program model fell short (in which case you should abandon that model), or were you unable to follow a proven model due to outside circumstances (in which case you may want to try again)?

◊ Look at all facets of the project – The best partnerships are designed with targeted outcomes for students, schools, and partners. Did your partnership fall short on all three fronts, or did you see successes that you can build on in one or two of those three areas?

◊ Share your outcomes anyway – Your partners and supporters need to know what happened, and will appreciate your forthright approach. Keep your focus on learning from the experience by sharing your analysis with them and telling them how you plan to change going forward. You may be surprised at how many stick with you when they see your commitment to producing positive outcomes and learning from experience.

Engaging Partners for the Long Haul

5.1 Partner Retention

In business, there's an old saying that it costs much more to get a new customer than it does to keep a current one. That's true in partnership work as well: When you think about the effort it takes to find a partner and persuade them to start working with you, it's easy to appreciate how valuable your current partners are, and how important it is to keep them.

Partner retention isn't just about minimizing costs, however. Partners increase in value the longer they stay with you. They start to understand how your school operates; they build long-term relationships with teachers and students; and they're more comfortable advocating for your work, spreading the messages to community leaders and to other businesses who might partner with you as well.

In 2010, DeHavilland Associates conducted a survey of school- and district-level partnership directors on partner retention. The results, published in the August 2010 issue of the *K-12 Partnership Report* newsletter, provide important insights into why partners leave, and what strategies work in keeping them.

Why Do Partnerships End?

Of course, some partnerships end entirely because of business reasons: A

Partnership Director Survey: Why Partnerships End			
Survey Item	**Not at all/not very frequent**	**Sometimes**	**Frequent/ very frequent**
Below are some common reasons why partnerships end. Please indicate how frequently these issues come up in your partnerships.			
School personnel have no time to manage partnerships properly	21.2%	40.0%	38.9%
There are no consequences for managing partnerships poorly	30.2%	36.0%	33.7%
Partnership did not track activity or outcomes; partner did not see results for their efforts	43.8%	32.6%	23.6%
Business is no longer operational or experiencing cutbacks	19.3%	58.0%	22.7%
School did not employ good partnership recognition strategies	39.8%	37.5%	22.7%
Transfer or promotion of CEO or designated business-site partnership coordinator	39.1%	39.1%	21.8%
Transfer or promotion of principal or designated school-based partnership coordinator	35.2%	44.3%	20.5%
School did not employ good retention strategies	37.1%	42.7%	20.2%
There is not enough district support	53.3%	27.8%	18.9%
Partnership did not meet partner needs	37.9%	51.7%	10.3%
Partner did not feel like an equal in the partnership; they were "outmanned"	64.8%	27.3%	7.9%
Principal is not supportive of community involvement	62.2%	32.2%	5.5%
Business is no longer interested	55.7%	39.8%	4.5%

business closes or experiences cutbacks or its priorities change in such a way that the partnership no longer makes sense. But according to the survey, there are also a lot of factors under the control of the school.

The main reason partnerships ended: Schools did not treat them as being important. Staff were not given the time needed to support the partnership; there were no consequences for poor management; or the school did not invest in the relationship, in terms of recognizing partners or focusing on partner retention.

According to the survey respondents, this often boils down to a leadership issue. Comments included:

> It is almost always true that those schools that frequently lose partners have a principal that does not value community involvement.

> It's about the people: The instructional leader (principal) has to encourage and support partnerships or teachers aren't going to take the time to invest in them.

> Partnerships are best with a strong and supportive principal at the school level and a responsive individual contact who handles day-to-day partner relations.

Partnership Director Survey: Retention Strategies

Survey Item	Ineffective/ somewhat ineffective	Somewhat effective	Effective/ very effective	Not applicable
Below are some strategies that school staff use for partnership retention. Please indicate how effective each strategy has been for your schools.				
School is a positive environment in which to work/volunteer	2.3%	9.1%	88.6%	0%
School recognizes their partners frequently and in a variety of ways	1.1%	11.4%	85.2%	2.3%
School deals with problems promptly	2.3%	11.5%	83.9%	2.3%
Staff makes it a priority to address partner needs/concerns	4.6%	10.3%	83.9%	1.1%
Schools and their partners communicate frequently	1.1%	14.8%	80.7%	3.4%
The principal stays engaged with partnerships	5.7%	12.6%	79.3%	2.3%
Needs of partners have been identified and are addressed	4.7%	15.1%	76.7%	3.5%
Partners know how they impact student achievement	6.8%	13.6%	71.6%	8.0%
Partner volunteers receive training	3.6%	14.1%	62.4%	20.0%
School provides their partners with outcome data on the effectiveness of activities in supporting student achievement	14.8%	17.0%	58.0%	10.2%
Partners receive orientation	5.7%	9.2%	57.5%	27.6%
School-based partnership coordinators hold an administrative position at school	4.6%	16.3%	40.7%	38.4%
Effective partnerships are part of the designated school-based partnership coordinator's annual review	4.6%	6.9%	39.0%	49.4%
A stipend is paid to the school-based partnership coordinator	11.4%	6.9%	18.3%	63.2%

Engaging Partners for the Long Haul

Self-Assessment

Think about the last three partners that decided to stop working with you. How many of those departures were for business reasons? How many could have been prevented if the school had done things differently?

While no one can prevent every partner from leaving, the consensus seems to be that schools are capable of retaining many of their partners if they make partnerships a priority.

Retention Strategies

Clearly, if schools make partnerships a priority, they can keep more of their partners involved in their schools. But what does it mean to make them a priority? What practical steps can you take?

The survey again provides some solid guidance. While there are several strategies considered to be effective, they can be summarized with four points:

◊ Make participation a positive experience for the businesspeople. Make sure the school feels like a positive environment, recognize your partners frequently, and treat them as important by taking their concerns seriously and responding quickly.

◊ Make sure school leaders stay engaged in some way. Make them visible among staff and businesspeople, and have them talk often about how important these partnerships are to their school.

◊ Let partners know that they're making a difference. Tell them how they're affecting student achievement, and share data on outcomes so they can see hard proof of their impact.

◊ Prepare partners for their role in the school; offer training or an orientation session as appropriate.

Survey respondents offered the following additional thoughts:

Consider them part of their school "family," inviting them to school events, adding them to e-mail newsletter mailing lists, etc.

Creating a general environment where partners feel welcomed and useful is the most effective way. Being really organized helps too. Last, student preparation is huge: Schools that are ineffective tend to not prepare students for successful interactions.

Partners understand exactly what their donations (time, money, etc.) are being used for.

To increase partner retention in your school, think about your most important partners and complete the worksheet on the following page.

Partnership Planning Worksheet: Partner Retention

Schools can have a huge influence on whether partners stay or go. Use this worksheet as a brainstorming tool to consider the strategies that might be most effective in keeping your most valuable partners.

---

1. What are three ways that I can make partnering a positive experience for this business?
Examples: Have a clean, orderly environment; teach children how to interact with volunteers; respond quickly when they call or email; make sure they get a lot of recognition

_____

_____

_____

2. How can I keep school leadership engaged in this relationship?
Examples: Make sure administrators understand the impact partners are having on student achievement, or the resources they're bringing to the school; have your principal sit on your advisory council

_____

_____

_____

3. What are two ways that I can show partners how important they are to our work?
Examples: Make sure they understand the goals of the partnership; track and share data on student outcomes

_____

_____

_____

4. What are three ways I can prepare businesspeople for the partnership?
Examples: Offer a volunteer orientation; give them a written volunteer guide; pair them with experienced partners at meetings; offer training in areas important to the project

_____

_____

_____

5.2 Recognizing Your Partners

Two of the most powerful words in the English language are "thank you."

Even though your partners aren't working with your school just to get a pat on the back, recognizing and thanking them still has a huge influence on how they think about the experience. If you want to keep partners engaged and coming back again and again, you should make sure they know how much you value their contribution.

Self-Assessment

Think back to some of your own experiences as a volunteer or donor.

◊ *Can you remember a time when you made a real effort to help, and were not thanked in any way? How did you feel about the experience? Did you want to come back and help some more?*

◊ *Think about a time when you supported an organization and they went out of their way to thank you. How did you feel about the experience? Did you want to come back and help some more?*

There are several ways to recognize your partners, many of which cost nothing:

◊ A personal thank you letter, not a blanket form letter, should be the very first thing you do to thank your donors. This could come from the lead teacher, the principal, or from an advisory board member. Consider having students write letters as well, detailing the impact the partnership has had on their lives.

◊ Plaques are a standard recognition tool. This could be a plaque sent to the partner to display at their place of business, or it could be a plaque displayed at the school. Consider creating a "Partners Wall" that lists all partners, perhaps at different levels such as platinum, gold, and silver. You could also do a variation on the plaque idea by instead ordering trophies that line up with the theme of the partnership.

◊ Take a photograph of the partnership in action; for example, photograph a volunteer or partner working with a student and send a framed copy of the photo to your partner.

◊ Provide a written update about the program's outcomes.

◊ Recognize your partner at a public event. This could be a school event, like a school-wide assembly or a school board meeting, or it could be at one of your partner's events.

◊ Host a reception or a dinner for all your partners. This way, you have a semi-public opportunity to show your thanks, and partners can mingle.

◊ Try to get press coverage of your partnership. Center your press release around something timely, tying it into current events or around an award won by students participating in the partnership.

◊ Use your internal communication channels. Post logos, photos, or articles in your school newsletter or on your website.

◊ Give the donor a memento of their work with you. If they're working with carpentry students, have the students build something for their office and surprise them with it. If they're working with a robotics team, have the team give them an early prototype for display.

◊ Create a "thank you" video showing the partnership in action, with teachers, students, and volunteers talking about the partnership and what it's meant to them.

Remember to involve your advisory board wherever possible. Make sure your board is represented at any event, and that it participates in your recognition efforts in some way. Including your partners' business peers in the recognition process will further increase the value of the effort.

Recognition Letter - Sample

Date

Name
Company
Address
City, State Zip

Dear NAME,

I'm writing to thank you for the leadership you have shown in establishing our career mentoring program, and your continued support in hosting students through that program.

Because of you and your company, 30 of our students have been able to gain firsthand experience in this industry, meeting and interacting with professionals and seeing for themselves how people work together in the workplace. We can work with them in the classroom to teach the technical skills, but we can't give them the kind of real-world exposure they need to understand industry expectations, and truly understand what it's like to work in the industry. Only partners like you can do that. And you've made a tremendous difference in the lives of these children and future employees.

We truly appreciate your work with our students and staff, and value your continued input on how we can make this partnership valuable to you and to our students. I look forward to continuing this work with you in the years to come.

Sincerely,

You

5.3 The Annual Review

Building a successful partnership is hard work: It takes vision, effort, and a sustained commitment from all parties to get it up and running. And once it's in motion, producing the results you and your partner had hoped for, it's easy to go on autopilot, slipping back into maintenance mode on your now-proven program while you look for other fires to put out.

But if you've got a successful partnership, autopilot may be the riskiest path you can take. Partnerships have lots of moving parts, and over time, circumstances can change. Your needs, or your partners' needs, may change; the goals of the partnership may become less important over time; or other solutions may rise up from other sources. Change can come from almost anywhere, making your initiative less effective or less relevant.

For that reason, it makes sense to sit down with your major partners on a regular basis to review your work together. Not only will this allow you to make sure your partnership continues to be effective, but it might also help you expand the program so you can make a greater impact.

Annual Review: Different from Measurement and Evaluation

The strategic review is different from your ongoing measurement and evaluation efforts. Measurement and evaluation are like the indicators on the dashboard of your car: They'll tell you how fast you're going and how much gas you have. But they won't tell you what's happening outside the car: They won't tell you whether it's snowing, or whether a bridge is out on the road ahead.

In order to make sure your program responds to the current state of the market — i.e., those external conditions outside the scope of your evaluation "dashboard" such as changes in the needs of your partner or your students — you need to sit down with your partner to hold an annual strategic review of your efforts.

Planning the Annual Review

An annual review is an opportunity to step back from day-to-day operations and review the work you've done to date, the landscape in which you operate, and whether you need a course correction in order to continue providing value to your stakeholders. You can hold a review more than once a year, which may be a good idea in areas experiencing rapid change, but at the very least you should look at doing this once per year, ideally in the spring or summer.

It's best to start planning for your strategic review several weeks prior to any sort of actual retreat: many of the questions you'll need to answer will require some research well before you begin brainstorming and strategizing on next steps. You'll also want that time to get feedback and insights from key figures involved in the partnership, including teachers, lead volunteers, students, and any other representatives of important stakeholder groups. Be sure to set the date several months in advance so your board members can reserve the time on their calendars.

Finally, be sure your partners have any needed supporting documents (like outcome data or financial statements) prior to your meeting; they'll appreciate having some time to review these kinds of materials.

Elements of the Strategic Review

Some of the big-picture items you should incorporate into your strategic review include:

<u>**Return on Investment**</u>
All of the stakeholders in your partnership chose to get involved because they felt it would help them achieve something that was important to them. This is a good time to ask: Are people's interests still the same, or have their priorities changed?

Suppose your partner started working with you to address an urgent workforce need, but one of their competitors closed and they now have access to a large group of people with the required skill sets. What does that mean for your partnership? What other needs do they have that you can address together? It may mean that the partnership stays the same, but that you measure a different outcome for your business partner; maybe your partner also cares about employee morale, and your partnership has benefits on that front as well. Or maybe it's time to revisit the kind of partnership you have so that it meets your partner's new set of needs.

<u>**Logic Model**</u>
A Logic Model, or Theory of Change, simply outlines how your partnership is intended to work (see Section IV for more on the Logic Model). When you launched your initiative, it was based on a logic model: You had a target population that you wanted to move from point A to point B, and you allocated resources and initiated some activities to create that change. It's time to take a fresh look at all of those elements.

◊   You designed your program to serve a specific population — is your target population still the correct one? The children (or other population) that you serve — are they still the right audience for your program?

◊   If your intervention is designed to move them from point A to point B, are they still starting from point A? Your program is designed to move program participants ahead in some way — have they moved ahead on their own through some other intervention (such as a change in the school curriculum), eliminating the need for intervention?

◊   Do they still need to get to point B? Have you seen any evidence that your desired outcome is no longer the right one? Has there been any new research indicating that children don't benefit from being proficient in the area you've selected?

◊   Is the axis of change still the correct one? The thing that you're working to improve, whether graduation rates, test scores, or something else — is it still relevant and important? Is there now a better way to define it, or a way to narrow your focus within that area to better target your efforts and create a greater impact?

◊   Is your intervention still the right way to achieve your goals effectively and efficiently? Has anything come to light, such as new research or new technology, that would allow you to better help program participants succeed? Are there new ways of operating that you should consider going forward?

Competition

No partnership operates in a vacuum: There are often alternatives available to your chosen audiences. When considering the services you offer to your target audience, consider whether there are any new organizations operating in your market or whether any existing organizations have expanded their service area or capabilities to become new (or better) competitors.

If new competition exists, how well are they meeting the needs of the market? If they're doing a good job, does it make sense to rethink your objectives and focus on an area that's not currently served? Are there opportunities for collaboration in order to avoid duplication of effort? Or can you work in a complementary way to better fill the needs of your constituents? How else can you differentiate yourself to provide clear and distinct benefits to your audience and to your stakeholders?

Asset mix

As sponsors and supporters come and go, the mix of assets available to fuel your efforts will change. What does this mean to your way of doing business? Have you lost certain types of resources that are expensive to replace — for example, do you now have to purchase materials that were once donated? Have you gained a new type of asset thanks to the addition of a new partner? This is the time to consider how your program aligns with your asset mix and, if there is a disconnect, to figure out ways to take full advantage of the resources currently available to you.

Feedback

Assuming you've been collecting feedback from program participants and supporters, what are they telling you about your program? This type of feedback, from people who have a vested interest in your work, is valuable and should be given due consideration.

Personnel

The strategic review is the perfect time to consider the human part of your program. Depending on what you want to achieve during the next year, you may need to staff up in some ways, either by getting more school support or boosting your volunteer base. This is also an opportunity to look at leadership, asking whether you have the right program leaders in place to continue moving ahead.

Growth

If you're achieving the kinds of results you intended, and if you've managed to build a sustainable enterprise, it may be time to consider a path to growth. This could take several forms, including:

◊   Expansion to different geographical markets

◊   Broadening your target audience — either serving more students or accepting other groups of students (different ages, different needs), making sure to accommodate them based on their differing characteristics as necessary

◊   Building on your list of targeted goals — adding new objectives, such as content, skill, behavioral, or attitudinal objectives, to the list of things you wish to accomplish

◊   Increasing the channels through which you operate — you may consider expanding to Web-based content delivery, a video series, published resources, or other ways of building new outlets to your desired market.

By stepping back to review all of the elements of your partnership, both internal and external, you'll not only ensure that your work remains relevant and vibrant, but also uncover opportunities to build on existing success — a far easier prospect than creating new programs from scratch.

Deep Dive: Advisory Boards

6.1 Advisory Board Basics

Advisory boards are an integral component of any educational program that seeks to engage employers, including career and technical education (CTE) programs as well as career academies, industry-focused charter schools (e.g., STEM schools), and the like. Advisory boards can come in a variety of formats, depending on the needs of the students, the structure of the school and district, and the make-up of the community at large.

As their name implies, advisory boards are typically formed to "advise" a school-based program. Areas of advisement typically include:

◊ Curriculum updates and collateral material

◊ Designing and setting up work-based learning activities

◊ Major projects or programs

◊ Professional development for teachers and staff

◊ Advocating on behalf of the school or program

◊ Interviewing new teachers for the program

◊ Assisting with aligning curriculum with current workforce needs and postsecondary offerings

◊ Fundraising

In the pages that follow, you will have an opportunity to think about and plan ways to engage your local business community in your program. You'll find charts, tables, templates, forms, and other resources to assist you in maximizing the benefits of engaging business leaders and, in doing so, providing life-changing learning experiences for your students.

Key Principles

There are some advisory board basics that, when applied and followed, will yield great benefits for your program and your students. These include:

Advisory boards must be made up largely of business leaders

The resources required by students, schools, and districts, including paid internships, scholarships, job shadowing, mentoring, classroom speakers, and other work-based learning activities, cannot come from school and district staff, teachers, counselors, or others from the learning community. They can only be provided by representatives from business (including large, national companies, and smaller, local companies) and the community at large (including two- and four-year postsecondary representatives).

Advisory boards should have active members

Advisory boards should have enough active members to provide (or find) the necessary human and financial resources required by your program. Typically, this means that the advisory board should have around 15–20 members, at least 75 percent of whom should be business members. It's often easier for CTE and other school-based people to recruit and work with school-based members on the advisory board. Examples of these school-based people include core academic teachers, counselors, the principal, assistant principal, someone from the district CTE office, etc. However, CTE and program directors who want to be able to provide the necessary resources to a program should recruit a large percentage of business people to the advisory board — people who are in a position to provide or find those resources.

The chart below represents the suggested makeup of the membership of an advisory board:

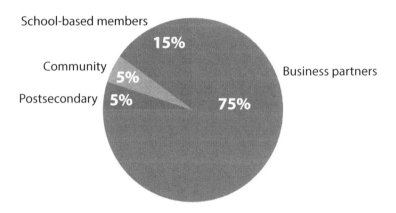

Business partners should actively run the advisory board

The officers of the advisory board should all be representatives from the business community, and the chair (or co-chairs) should run the meetings. Although it is tempting for the CTE or program director (a school-based person) to run the board meetings, experience has shown that more-successful advisory boards are

Setting Program Goals

The table below can be used to identify annual goals for your program (Col 1), the timeline for when those goals need to be completed (Col 2), who will be responsible for making sure the goals are being completed in a timely fashion (Col 3), and key measurements or benchmarks that can be used during the allotted time period to check progress (Col 4).

The partner(s) named in the "Who" column is(are) primarily responsible for actually completing the goal. This will include not only planning the processes and procedures for accomplishing the goal, but also determining who the partner(s) need to recruit (from within the advisory board, the school/district, and from the community at large) to achieve the goal within the allotted time frame.

	What needs to be done (primary goals)	**When** must we be done (completion date)	**Who** is responsible (committee chair/others)	**How** do we know we're making progress (benchmarks/milestones)
1				
2				
3				
4				

Deep Dive: Advisory Boards

run by representatives who work in the business world, know how to talk with and motivate the other business-based members of the advisory board, and have the leader qualities and experience necessary to actively engage the rest of the advisory board members.

Put your advisory board to work

One of the key principles of working successfully with business partners is to have very specific goals and timelines. Business partners are used to having goals, deadlines, benchmarks, quotas, budgets, and the like each and every day in their business dealings. Providing similar goals and timelines in their volunteer work with schools motivates partners to engage, grow, and sustain their involvement.

Put business partners in positions of strength

Another key principle of working successfully with business partners is to put each partner in a position of strength. That means identifying their innate talents, preferences, interests, propensities, and positive skill sets, and then putting them in a position to capitalize on those strengths when working on your advisory board and with your program.

The chart below may be helpful not only in identifying existing partner strengths to work best with your advisory board (work table left to right), but also in finding the right new people when recruiting new members to your advisory board (work table right to left).

See table and examples below:

Name	Email/Phone	Strengths/Talents/ Interests	Best Role on Advisory Board
Beverly Jones	bjones@gmail.com 555-555-5555	Likes to talk on the phone, knows a lot of community members, doesn't mind hearing "No", persistent, tenacious, empathetic, communicative, excellent presentation skills	Fundraising committee member
Steve Smith	ssmith@yahoo.com 555-555-5556	Has many contacts in community, involved with Rotary, Chamber of Commerce, Lions, Knights of Columbus, other professional or service organizations, fully understands how a work-based learning experience motivates students, not afraid to "close the sale"	Chair of internship committee

<u>Let your board members assume responsibility</u>

Since business partners are used to taking responsibility for completing goals at work, the most successful advisory boards assume full responsibility for completing the goals agreed to in the beginning of the school year. For example, if your junior class consists of 50 students who need a paid internship the following summer, the internship committee of the advisory board should be presented with that goal early in the school year (August time frame) and should then assume full responsibility for "furnishing, funding, or finding" those 50 internship positions. The internship committee should be prepared at each advisory board meeting to report out on their progress to date.

Resource Links

The following links provide good information on building and managing advisory boards:

◊   http://naf.org/resources-list/business-partners

◊   http://naf.org/resources/advisory-board-storymap-pdf

◊   http://naf.org/files/AB_Manual_2009_update_9-30.pdf

◊   http://www.ncacinc.com/academies

◊   http://casn.berkeley.edu/

6.2 Advisory Board Structure

The effectiveness of your advisory board will be influenced by how well you define the roles of your board members, how you structure your board, and where your board is located within your school or district. Setting these up correctly at the outset will help things run more smoothly over the life of your board.

Defining Leadership Roles

Whether you're launching a new board or reinvigorating an existing one, one of your first priorities should be to clearly define leadership roles and the responsibilities of all board members. This will help you make sure that all important tasks are being covered, and that people new to their positions clearly understand what's expected of them.

The following lists detail responsibilities common to each position. You'll want to start with a list similar to one of those below, customize it based on your vision for each role, and include specific details wherever possible.

Chairperson

The chairperson of the advisory board has a critical role to play in the success of the program. He or she ensures that the board functions properly, that there is full and active participation in meetings, that board members are able to hold full and open discussions, and that effective decisions are made and carried out.

Responsibilities of the chairperson include:

◊ Ensure that the advisory board functions properly, including:

» Planning and running meetings according to guidelines

» Running meetings in an orderly, efficient manner

» Ensuring that important issues are raised, that board members have an opportunity to discuss them openly and honestly, and that differing opinions and perspectives are encouraged

» Maintaining the board's focus on the effectiveness of the program, including tracking outcomes and overseeing progress on board initiatives

◊ Ensure that the advisory board is managed effectively, including:

» Working with the head of the program to stay informed about the program's efforts and to coordinate the efforts of the advisory board accordingly

» Coordinating with other board members to ensure responsibilities are fulfilled and that goals (including committee goals) are met

» Overseeing the advisory board's talent pipeline, identifying possible new board members, and seeing that current members have an opportunity to move into leadership positions

◊ Represent the program, including:

» Participating in industry events as a representative of the program

» Participating in meetings and phone calls with prospective business partners and funders

» Speaking with teachers and students as head of the advisory board about the interests and needs of the business community

Secretary

The secretary of the advisory board supports effective board operations by capturing information at meetings and making sure members have access to notes and information critical to board efforts. He or she is also responsible for logistics, such as scheduling and setting up meetings. The role of the secretary may vary based on the availability of support from program staff.

Responsibilities of the secretary include:

◊ Preparing meeting agendas and supporting documentation in consultation with the chairperson and other board members

◊ Circulating relevant materials prior to meetings

◊ Scheduling meetings and ensuring board members and other invited guests have advance notice

◊ Checking that a quorum is present for any votes

◊ Taking minutes of the meetings and circulating drafts to board members

◊ Keeping up-to-date records of board activities and any organizational mandates (state filings, etc.)

Treasurer

The treasurer of the advisory board maintains an overview of the board's financial affairs, manages any associated financial operations, and is responsible for any required financial reporting.

Responsibilities of the treasurer include:

◊ Preparing and presenting budgets, financial statements, and other related reports to the board

◊ Working with program staff on financial matters as appropriate, including advising on the financial implications of new projects or other initiatives

◊ Ensuring that appropriate accounting procedures are in place and that all financial processes are in compliance with school mandates

◊ Handling finances, including receipt of payments and vendor management, for any board projects or activities

In addition to these three key positions, you may also wish to outline other important roles, such as the position of vice chairperson (which will draw heavily from the chairperson description) and any committee chair roles you decide to create.

Boards and Committees

There is no one correct way to structure an advisory board. One school may have a single board assuming all functions, while another may have a more complicated structure, with committees and subcommittees focused on specific areas. To decide how to structure your board, consider the following common board and committee models:

◊ **Strategic Executive Board** – This is the "master board" on which all of your board members sit. It is responsible for high-altitude oversight, providing strategic guidance and community feedback and serving as a point of connection for the larger community.

◊ **Regional Industry Sector Committee** – A broader-level committee that helps you link your efforts to a specific industry cluster in your region, gathering information on current and future industry needs and workforce trends so you can align your efforts accordingly.

◊ **Program Advisory Committee** – A narrower committee intended to support specific programs with the insights and perspectives of employers in that field, allowing you to tailor learning objectives and curriculum to industry standards and needs.

◊ **Occupational/Industry Advisory Committee** – Distinct from the regional industry sector committee in that it is more tactical and program-specific. This committee is still focused on gathering industry information and trends, looking at changes in the market so you know what employers need now and in the future.

◊ **Other Committees or Subcommittees** – Depending on your needs, you may also consider the following as committees or subcommittees:

  » **Postsecondary Transitions** – Making sure your outcomes line up with postsecondary entrance requirements

  » **Recruiting** – If you need to attract students to your program

» **Talent Development** – Focused on staff and student development opportunities

» **Facilities and Equipment** – Concentrating on overseeing major fundraising or acquisition efforts

» **Communications/Advocacy** – Serving as the public face of your program

» **Program Accreditation** – Aligning your programs to accreditation requirements

One strategy for designing your structure is to identify your board leadership, or at least your chairperson, and asking them to participate in identifying board functions and structure.

Boards Within a School/District Structure

If you have a single program with a single advisory board, it's easy to envision how the board relates to its program. But how should you structure your board(s) if you have several programs, or several schools within a district that may have some overlapping programs? One common concern, for example, is that several schools are all asking the same local businesses to participate on their board, leading that partner to sit on five different boards, each covering very similar ground.

Consider the following structures to decide what works for your program, school, and/or district:

One school/one program

One school/multiple programs, option 1: Multiple boards

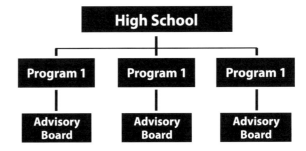

One school/multiple programs, option 2: Single board

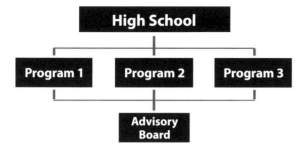

Multiple schools/multiple local school-based boards

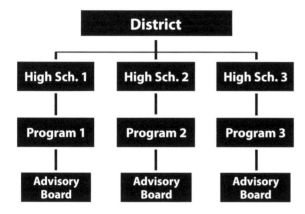

Multiple schools/multiple programs, with one overarching district-wide executive board and multiple local school-based boards

◊ Executive board handles some common functions for all programs in district, such as aligning curriculum to workforce needs and community outreach/advocacy

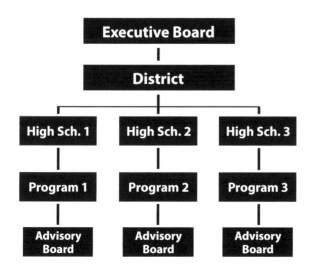

6.3 Building Your Advisory Board

When you hired staff for your program, you thought carefully about your needs and what kinds of people could do the jobs you needed to have done. Recruiting members for your board is no different: You'll need people with the right skills and experience to accomplish the goals that you set together.

Finding the Right Mix

You want your board to accomplish a lot, which means that your board members collectively must have the experience, connections, skills, and drive needed to complete the tasks they agree to take on. *Collectively* is an important concept: No one board member has to be able to do everything. Instead, different people will bring different skills and assets to the table.

Make sure that, as a whole, your board members cover the following bases:

◊ Connect you with key stakeholder groups such as businesses, industry groups, and community leaders (including political, postsecondary, and civic) to let them know about your program and recruit them as partners and supporters

◊ Identify opportunities within their own organizations and others for work-based learning opportunities for students as well as professional development opportunities for staff

◊ Provide an independent, industry-oriented perspective so they can tell you what opportunities exist, or will exist, for students, and what skills and knowledge students will need to attain those opportunities

◊ Provide management expertise to assist with oversight and planning functions, and to help with any particular priorities you've set such as branding, fundraising, outreach, or facilities development

Recruiting

As stated previously, your advisory board membership should be composed of about 75 percent business leaders. Starting from scratch may be the most difficult assignment for a CTE or school-based program leader. Venturing out into the business community to recruit new members can be quite challenging for someone who does not have business experience. Some good places to start include:

◊ Chamber of commerce – Set up an appointment to speak with the chair of the education committee, workforce development committee, or member volunteer committee.

◊ Parents of your students who work in the same industry as your program

◊　Business section of your Sunday newspaper – Contact people highlighted in the "Movers and Shakers" section, people noted or photographed in the "Benefits or Galas" section, or people who write letters or opinion pieces on workforce issues.

◊　Rotary, Kiwanis, Lions, Elks, or other local service or volunteer organizations – Take a student to meet with people involved in community volunteerism.

◊　Professional associations – See the chair of the community involvement, member volunteer, or workforce departments of a professional association connected to your program's theme, such as a banker's association, engineering association, or hospitality association.

◊　Companies in your program's industry that have a large office or plant in your community – Ask for the human resources department, and speak with someone in the employee volunteerism or community engagement area.

◊　Other companies unrelated to your program's theme – Excellent resources can come from public utility companies, hospitals, and local government agencies.

◊　Other teachers or administrators at your school or district may have personal or professional connections that can help.

◊　Higher education institutions, both two year and four year, should be represented on your board; they may also have industry contacts serving either as volunteers or as members of their own programs' advisory boards.

It helps to remember that workforce preparedness is the greatest area of interest for business partners who think about working with schools, as seen in the chart at the bottom of this page.

Survey of Business Leaders: What Types of Partnership Outcomes Are Most Important?

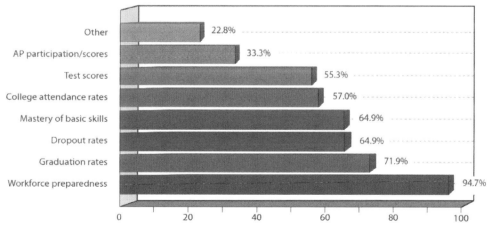

Source: DeHavilland Associates, 2007

Once you've identified and recruited your first couple of board members, they can then take over responsibility for finding and recruiting the rest of your advisory board. Sometimes you really only need one good advisory board member to create a cascade of new, motivated, engaged, and productive members. You might also decide to set up a standing recruiting/membership committee, and remind all others that they should be on the lookout for new members to keep the board at full capacity. Remember, putting your board members to work keeps them motivated and engaged.

What to Look for in a Board Member

While professional affiliations are important, an effective board requires that members have certain personal skill sets and characteristics as well. You'll want

Recruitment Letter - Sample

Name
Title
Company
Street Address
City, State, Zip

Dear First Name;

As Chair of the Advisory Board Recruitment Committee for the (career/technical/work-based/academy) program at _____ High School, I am writing to invite you to join other leaders from the business community on the program's Advisory Board. The _____ program is available to high school students who have expressed or shown an interest in, or a propensity for, certain college and career paths.

The program combines rigorous core academic classes with industry-related, work-based learning classes focusing on career awareness, exploration, preparation, and application. A large majority of graduates from this program go on to college and careers in the related industry.

Since you are a leader in this industry, you can make an important impact on the future of the students. By sharing a small amount of your time, expertise, knowledge, and business acumen, you can open students' eyes to the many career opportunities within the _____ industry.

Please consider attending the next Advisory Board meeting of the _____ program. By meeting the other Advisory Board members already involved, and seeing the professional interaction between business leaders, school personnel, and students, you'll get a first-hand look at the impact you can make on the students.

The next meeting will be held on (date) at (time) at (location). Please RSVP by calling me directly at (phone). At that time, I can also answer any questions you might have about the program, the Advisory Board, your prospective involvement, and the likely time commitment.

Thank you very much for considering this invitation.

Sincerely,

_____
Chair – Recruitment Committee
Program, High School
Title, Company
E-mail, Phone

people with the experience and skills needed to be able to represent their community affiliations; this means that you'll want people with at least five to 10 years of experience, not people fresh out of school. You'll want people with established professional networks, access to resources, and the personal skills to work in a board environment, including interpersonal skills, time, and passion.

Bringing Members on Board

It's an honor to be asked to sit on an advisory board; it's also a significant commitment. Both sides of this equation need to be considered when inviting others to serve on your board.

When you make the request, treat it with the importance it deserves. Invest in your new relationship by bringing along a senior board member, like your chairperson, and take the time to visit your prospective member's workplace to learn more about what their organization does. Some CTE leaders note that they will spend a few hours taking a tour and meeting others at these organizations (an investment that can pay dividends later in the form of new relationships).

Let your prospective member know what you're trying to accomplish, and why it's important for the students, the industry, and the community. They'll want to know they're being asked to invest their time in something worthwhile. At the same time, spell out specifically what the commitment entails: How many meetings there are and when they're held, as well as what members are

---

Termination Letter - Sample

Date

Name
Title
Company
Address
City, State, Zip

Dear First Name,

Thank you very much for your service to the students of _____ High School while serving as a member of the Advisory Board. As Chair of the Advisory Board for the _____ program at _____ High School, I regret to inform you that you have not met the minimum expectations and parameters required to continue your role as an Advisory Board member as outlined in the By-laws of the Advisory Board.

Accordingly, your membership on the Advisory Board will be terminated at (time) on (date). No further action is necessary on your part. However, if you'd like the Advisory Board to reconsider this termination, please contact me at (e-mail address) or (phone) to discuss your options.

Thank you again for your service to the students of _____ High School, and your dedication to improving the education of young people.

Sincerely,

Advisory Board Chair
E-mail, Phone

Resignation Letter - Sample

To: Advisory Board Chair

Date

Title
Company
Street Address
City, State, Zip

Dear Advisory Board Chair,

I regret to inform you that I must resign my position as a member of the Advisory Board for _____ program at _____ High School. My (work schedule, personal life, other) is interfering with my ability to devote the time and resources necessary to continue to be a productive member of the Advisory Board.

Accordingly, I hereby resign from the Advisory Board effective (time) on (date). Please feel free to contact me at (email address) or (phone) if you'd like to further discuss the details of my decision.

Thank you for allowing me to serve the students of _____ High School.

Sincerely,

Advisory Board Member
E-mail, Phone

---

expected to do (spend additional time on committees, represent the program at area meetings, etc.).

You'll want to have a written description of the responsibilities of board members and additional information for any key positions (chair, vice chair, committee head, etc.). If they're a good fit, the odds are strong that you'll soon be welcoming a new member to your board.

Termination and Resignation

Sometimes an advisory board member cannot effectively perform his or her duties. Work schedules, personal matters, business travel, etc., may preclude the member from regularly attending meetings, working on goals, presenting in classrooms, participating in events, etc. At some point, the advisory board member must consider resigning from the advisory board, or the advisory board must consider removing the member from the advisory board. The policies and procedures for terminating advisory board membership should be clearly spelled out in the advisory board by-laws.

6.4 Advisory Board Operations

More formal advisory boards work better than less formal boards. A less formal advisory board works more like a loose social organization or club, and has more problems with turnover and long-term commitment. A more formal board creates a membership structure, protocols, and procedures that promote active, engaged, productive involvement of members. Attributes of a more formal advisory board include:

By-laws

A more formal advisory board will have written by-laws that help to maintain structures, policies, procedures and protocols of the board. By-laws address such issues as terms for officers, succession policies, termination rules, and other issues that can be emotional or challenging to the CTE or program director. A good example of advisory board by-laws may be found on the website for the National Academy Foundation at http://naf.org/files/NAF_Advisory_Board_By-Laws_template.pdf.

Monthly meetings

While many states mandate a minimum number of CTE advisory board meetings per year, the most successful advisory boards meet monthly, on the same day and at the same time each month. For example, the advisory board meeting can be scheduled for the third Thursday of every month, at 8:00 a.m. That way, board members can block out the time on their business calendars for the whole year, and work the rest of their business meetings during the year around that pre-committed time.

Efficient scheduling

Advisory board meetings should always start and end on time: Remember that business leaders have scheduled their day around the advisory board meeting so it's important to respect their commitment. The meeting should be scheduled to start early in the day so business leaders come to the meeting first, before going to their offices. The meeting should always start on time, work briskly through the agenda, and conclude and adjourn on time. That way, business leaders are more likely to show up and participate knowing they can count on the meeting being productive and that they will be able to go on with their regular business day on schedule.

Written agenda and minutes

The secretary of the advisory board should prepare and distribute a written agenda for each meeting at least a week before the upcoming meeting. The secretary should also keep minutes of every meeting, and distribute those minutes no later than one week after the meeting takes place. Finally, the secretary should keep a current list of members, and update the list (for terminations and new members) at each advisory board meeting.

Example: Carencro High School Advisory Board By-Laws

Note: These are the by-laws of the advisory board for the Carencro, Louisiana High School Academy of Information Technology. You can use this as a guide in developing by-laws for your own advisory board.

ARTICLE 1 - NAME

The name of this board shall be the Carencro High School Academy of Information Technology Advisory Board ("Advisory Board").

ARTICLE II - PURPOSE

An Advisory Board functions in an advisory capacity to a local member Academy program of the National Academy Foundation (NAF). The Advisory Board follows the guidelines as promulgated in the NAF Academy Frameworks, providing Program Support, Advocacy and Organization services. Accordingly, the Advisory Board makes recommendations regarding the expansion of Academy programs, number of students and school districts, curriculum, teacher training, advocacy and budget. The Advisory Board also assists with raising funds, recruiting students, securing internships and scholarships, and providing in-kind contributions to the local Academy program. Further services provided by Advisory Board may be found in the Partnership Framework.

ARTICLE III - OBJECTIVES

The primary objective of the Advisory Board is to support the following goals and policies of the local Academy program:

- Providing support services for the Academy program and students
- Preparing Academy students through course work and related experiential education for the world of work and higher education.
- Providing paid internships for Academy students.
- Providing training opportunities for teachers.
- Soliciting assistance from the business community in funding the Academy program.
- Advocating on behalf of the local program to individuals and businesses within the industry and community
- Enlisting the expertise of individuals in the industry to assist with the development and evaluation of curriculum, student selection, scholarships, advocacy and internships.

ARTICLE IV - ORGANIZATION

The Advisory Board will meet monthly, eleven times per year (August through June). A bi-monthly or quarterly meeting schedule may be implemented after the Board is up and running for several years, at the discretion of the Board. Additional meetings by various Committees may be held from time to time, in order to give counsel and solve specific problems dealing with fundraising, internships, curriculum and other matters related to the Academy program.

ARTICLE V - MEMBERSHIP

Section 1. Membership:
1. The members of the Advisory Board shall be representatives of the technology industry, community leaders and educators. One or two student representative(s) shall be made ex-officio member(s.)
2. The Advisory Board shall consist of at least ten members not representing K-12 Education.
3. Members of the Advisory Board shall receive no compensation for their services as Advisory Board members.

Section 2. Term of Membership:
1. Members of the Advisory Board will serve a three year term.
2. Any member may resign from the Advisory Board by giving written notice to the Chairperson. The resignation will be effective immediately upon receipt of such notice. Board members forced to resign their positions shall make every effort to find a suitable replacement at their company.
3. Any member of the Advisory Board who shall fail to attend a minimum of three (3) advance notice meetings of the Advisory Board in any fiscal year may be asked to resign from the Advisory Board. A member will be deemed to have attended a meeting if a duly qualified substitute attends on behalf of the member. It shall be the responsibility of the absent Board member, to obtain the minutes of the missed meeting, and any materials disseminated at that meeting from the Academy Director.
4. Appointment will be for a term of three (3) years, which may be renewed by two-thirds vote of the members of the Advisory Board.

Section 3. Membership Requirements:
1. The selection of members shall be made without respect to race, color, creed, national origin, age, handicap, sexual orientation or gender. The Advisory Board shall include, but not be limited to, representatives from the following three broad categories: (1) the technology industry including individuals indirectly involved in the industry (i.e. IT department personnel from a local hospital), (2) the educational community, and (3) the community at large, including parents, students, colleges, universities, non-profit organizations, etc.
2. Candidates must be nominated by a member in good standing of the Advisory Board and approved by a two-thirds majority vote by its members.
3. Candidates must commit and/or assist with raising

funds for the local Academy program.

4. Candidates must demonstrate a willingness to commit to obtaining at least two (2) student internship positions at their firm or elsewhere.
5. Candidates must commit to providing in-kind contributions that will directly benefit the students in the local Academy program.

Section 4. Membership Year: Fiscal

ARTICLE VI - RESPONSIBILITIES

1. Commit to and/or assist with raising funds.
2. Secure internships.
3. Provide in-kind contributions.
4. Establish scholarships.
5. Strengthen public relations and publicity relative to the program.
6. Assist in evaluating the relevance and effectiveness of the curriculum to meet the needs of the industry.
7. Provide staff development activities for Academy teachers and the Academy Director.

ARTICLE VII - MEETINGS

Section 1. Quorum
A majority of the Advisory Board members shall constitute a quorum for conducting Advisory Board business.

Section 2. Voting
Each active member of the Advisory Board shall be entitled to vote on any issue presented to the Advisory Board. A duly qualified alternate in attendance at a meeting may vote on behalf of a member, but no proxy votes are allowed.

Section 3. Minutes
The Chairperson will designate a person to record and distribute the minutes to all Advisory Board members. The Academy Director will assist the Chairperson in coordinating the meetings and developing the agenda. The Academy Director will also ensure that absent Advisory Board members will receive material and minutes distributed at the Board meetings.

Section 4. Protocol
The Board meetings shall be run by the Chairperson or Vice/Co-Chairperson. The Academy Director's role shall be limited to reporting on the "state of the Academy program", and such other information as is necessary for the Board to carry out its advisory capacity. The Board Chairperson and Academy Director shall determine who (the school or the Board) is responsible for various tasks (preparing agendas, preparing and disseminating minutes, sending announcements, etc.), to avoid redundancies or delays in completing work assignments and achieving desired goals.

ARTICLE VIII - OFFICERS

Section 1. Chairperson
The Advisory Board shall consist of one Chairperson. The Chairperson shall be elected by the members of the Advisory Board every three (3) years. The elections will be held one year prior to the completion of the standing Chairperson's three year term.

Section 2. Vice Chairperson (Co-Chairperson)
The Advisory Board shall consist of one Vice or Co-Chairperson. The Vice or Co-Chairperson shall be elected by the members of the Advisory Board every three (3) years. The elections will be held one year prior to the completion of the standing Chairperson's three year term.

Section 3. Other Officers
Other officer positions such as Secretary and sub-committee chairpersons shall be decided by the majority of the Advisory Board members.

Section 4. Ex Officio Members
Ex officio members shall consist of selected industry leaders, state or municipal government officials and school district staff and students and are non-voting members.

Section 5. Elections
Elections will be held during the last meeting of the fiscal year.

ARTICLE IX - DUTIES OF THE OFFICERS

Section 1. Chairperson
The Chairperson's duties shall be those usually pertaining to the office as set forth in Robert's Rules of Order and such other duties as may be prescribed.

Section 2. Vice or Co-Chairperson
The Vice or Co Chairperson's duties shall be to direct all meetings in the absence of, or by agreement with the Chairperson to ensure the development and maintenance of a strong and active Advisory Board.

Section 3. Other Officers
Other officers' duties shall be those usually pertaining to the office as set forth in Robert's Rules of Order and such other duties as may be prescribed.

ARTICLE X - AMENDMENTS
These by-laws may be altered, amended, or repealed. New by-laws may be adopted by a majority vote of the Advisory Board at any regular meeting or special meeting.

By-laws provided courtesy of the Carencro High School Advisory Board, the Carencro High School Academy of Information Technology, and the Lafayette Parish School System Office of Schools of Choice.

Meeting Schedules

Meetings have a formal start time and end time and usually run between one and one-and-a-half hours long, following a consistent sequence such as the following:

◊ The chair (or co-chairs) opens and runs the meeting.

Advisory Board Meeting - Sample Agenda

Miami-Dade County Public Schools
Academy Advisory Board
May 1, 2014, 9:00 a.m.
Location: Smith & Wollensky

Welcome ....[Board Member]
Sagemark Sales & Marketing

Greetings ....[Board Member]
Smith & Wollensky
....[Board Member]
FRLA

MECA Report ....[Board Member]
ROI Media Consultants
Minutes ....[Board Member]
Johnson & Wales University

Progress Reports
A. Standing Committees (Strategic Plan)

1. Fundraising Committee ....[Board Member]
Launerts Hospitality Group

2. Governance & Membership Committee ....[Board Member]
Florida National University

3. Marketing & Communications Committee ....[Board Member]
EDF Communications

4. Student/Staff Development ....……[Board Member]
Black Hospitality Initiative of Greater Miami

B. Special Committee
1. Nominating Committee ....[Board Member]

District Update ....[Board Member]
Miami –Dade County Public Schools

Site Reports ....[Board Member]
Miami-Dade County Public Schools

New Business

Adjournment

This agenda provided by Miami Dade County Public Schools, Department of Career & Technical Education.

◊ There is a written agenda for the meeting that keeps the meeting on track and on time.

◊ Formal minutes are kept by the secretary, and distributed within a week of the meeting.

◊ The member roster is updated (for new and retiring advisory board members) monthly by the secretary.

◊ The treasurer reports out on the financials for the month (money in, money out, balance in account).

◊ Every committee chair has 5–6 minutes to report out on their progress toward achieving their goals (number of internships found, money raised, activities planned, etc.).

◊ A student representative (or two) gives a "state of the classroom" report, including student "needs and wants" (5 minutes).

◊ The program director gives a "state of the program/school" report (5–7 minutes).

◊ New business projects, issues, enrichment ideas, etc. are discussed (5–10 minutes).

◊ Other items are discussed, as appropriate (5–10 minutes).

◊ The meeting is adjourned at the planned time (or before –— never later).

By keeping meetings on track and on time, members know what to expect from month to month, and are more likely to show up regularly and participate fully.

Running Productive Meetings

Like most things, planning and preparation are the keys to running effective meetings and to running an effective board. You'll want to schedule meetings well in advance, ideally making up a calendar for the entire year and distributing it at the outset. You'll also want to make sure people have all the materials they need well in advance if they're expected to have reviewed them prior to your gathering.

When it comes to the meeting itself, be sure you're the first to arrive, and that you check out the technology beforehand (nothing slows down a meeting more than a projector with a burned-out bulb) and put out refreshments. During the meeting, get administrative details out of the way quickly, and manage the meeting purposefully: Allow discussions to go on as long as they're on point, but redirect or shut down unproductive tangents. Hold people accountable for their deliverables. And finally, without stretching out the official agenda, look for opportunities for people to socialize; for many businesspeople, board meetings are valuable opportunities to network with peers they may not see otherwise.

After your meeting, be sure to get meeting minutes out, and confirm assignment of any action items. If anyone was absent, do your best to bring them up to speed, sending out minutes and perhaps placing a phone call. And finally, confirm the date and location of your next meeting, giving everyone ample notice so they can plan for their participation.

Follow Robert's Rules of Order

Formal boards should follow Robert's Rules of Order in terms of calling meetings to order, having majority voting, establishing officers, having by-laws, etc. See www.robertsrules.org for more details. Examples of Robert's Rules include:

§	Purpose	You Say:	Interrupt?	Second?	Debate?	Amend?	Vote?
§21	Close meeting	I move to adjourn	No	Yes	No	No	Majority
§18	Call to follow the agenda	I call for the orders of the day	Yes	No	No	No	None
§16	Close debate	I move the previous question	No	Yes	No	No	2/3
§15	Limit/extend debate	I move that debate be limited to. . .	No	Yes	No	Yes	2/3
§10	Bring business before assembly	I move that. . .	No	Yes	Yes	Yes	Majority

6.5 Advisory Boards in the Long Term

It's not enough to focus on the day-to-day effectiveness of your advisory board: It's also important to step back and look at the big picture, and to think in the longer term about how you manage relationships and keep your board active and energized.

Strategic Reviews

A strategic review of your program should occur annually, usually in mid to late August or early September. This critical exercise provides a road map for the ensuing year for all stakeholders, and helps to set and prioritize goals. Prior to the strategic review, program leaders/directors should speak with all the school-based stakeholders (program teachers, counselors, principal or assistant principal, and a cadre of junior and seniors in the program) and compile a list of needs and wants (goals) as well as the estimated cost of satisfying those goals.

Strategic Review - Sample Agenda

8:30	Welcome/Introductions – The program director and advisory board chair open and run the meeting
8:40	Meeting Protocols – Outcomes, Roles, and Rules – Make sure meeting goals are clear, that everyone has an opportunity to contribute and participate, no one dominates, and everyone has fun
9:00	Academy Update – program director
9:15	Strategic Planning – Putting Things in Context – Internal trends, external trends, political climate, economic climate, technology factors, customer needs (who are our customers?), uncertainties.
10:15	Where Do We Want to Go? The Vision Quest – "Begin with the End in Mind" – Covey
11:00	Where Are We Now? – What's working, what's not working?
11:30	Priority Issues/SWOT Analysis
12:00	Lunch
1:00	How Will We Get There? – What do we have to do to achieve our goals?
2:00	Frameworks/Achieving Our Vision/Goal setting – Are we set up (structured) to achieve our goals, do we have the right people? What are our time frames? How do we know when we are achieving some success?
2:30	Who Will Do What?/TOES6 in Alignment (Time frame, Organization, Environment, Strategy, Structure, Systems, Staff, Style, Spirit)
3:00	How Are We Doing? – Benchmarks, short-term goals
3:15	What's Next? – Do we have joint agreement and clarity? Does everyone know his/her next steps? Is everyone committed to the success of the program?
3:30	Adjourn

For example, if a senior project is on the table, the program director should approximate the cost of materials, transportation, equipment, and other needed resources.

The strategic review meeting should take place at the school, should include all advisory board members and all learning community stakeholders, and should run for at least four hours and preferably a whole day. The agenda should be written and distributed well in advance of the meeting. The key to a successful strategic review is to have an open, frank, nonthreatening discussion about the program: What went well last year, what could be improved upon, what are the goals for the upcoming school year, and how can the advisory board support those goals. This is not a time for "finger-pointing" or "gotcha'" statements. Rather, it is a time for a pivotal dialogue to "peel back the layers of the onion" and have a realistic review of where the program is now, and where you want to take it.

A helpful tool when working through a strategic review is a SWOT diagram. SWOT (Strengths, Weaknesses, Opportunities, and Threats) provides a visual recap of the program's current status (Strengths and Weaknesses) and future issues (Opportunities and Threats). A sample SWOT diagram follows:

Strengths *What's working* ◊ Item ◊ Item ◊ Item	**Opportunities** *Where we can thrive* ◊ Item ◊ Item ◊ Item
Weaknesses *What's not working* ◊ Item ◊ Item ◊ Item	**Threats/Barriers** *What could keep us from our goals* ◊ Item ◊ Item ◊ Item

Since strategic planning is a very regular activity in the business community, it may be helpful for one of your advisory board members to provide a volunteer from his/her company (not the advisory board member) to facilitate the day-long discussion. Alternatively, you might try getting a volunteer from the Chamber of Commerce to facilitate the meeting. Either way, such a person may help to keep the meeting on track without letting any biases or personal issues get in the way.

Long-Term Viability

One of the major challenges of developing, growing, and managing an effective advisory board is paying attention to its sustainability. After a couple of years, even the most fervent members can succumb to boredom and burnout. This in turn can lead to the retirement of your best advisory board members, leaving your advisory board or your program in jeopardy. Knowing this ahead of time, and planning for these contingencies, minimizes the risk but also provides a written plan in the event a key member of your advisory board leaves.

Succession plan

A formal succession plan can be part of your advisory board by-laws, or can be a separate document. The purpose of a formal succession plan is to recognize that change is inevitable and, in the event an advisory board member must resign from your advisory board, there is a replacement protocol in place. This could include requiring a certain amount of notice (maybe 1–2 months) before the formal resignation is accepted. It could also provide that the resigning member is responsible for replacing him/herself with another representative from his/her organization. In any case, having a plan in place minimizes disruptions.

Refresh business partners' involvement activities

Consider changing the roles of business partners annually or biannually. For example, someone who is very good at fundraising might be the fundraising committee chair for a term of 2 years. After that, perhaps they move to the activities committee, or the internship committee. Changing roles requires your partners to learn new skills, talk with new people, and set new goals. In doing so, it keeps their interest fresh and their involvement exciting.

Term limits for Officers

Giving all board members the opportunity to chair committees and perhaps have an executive role on the advisory board keeps people interested and motivated. By limiting the terms of your officers, others can aspire to lead your advisory board, knowing that in a year or two, they could be elected to prominent positions. You can limit officers' terms in your by-laws. Consider "staggering" the terms of your officers as well so there isn't a "turnover" of the entire officer group at the same time or in the same year.

Recognize and celebrate all "wins"

It is very rare when a business person gets a "thank you" letter from a customer, supervisor, or business collaborator in the course of their normal business day. When a business partner volunteers his/her time, and makes an impact on your program or students (speaks in a classroom, hosts a job shadowing, provides an internship), a small expression of gratitude can go a long way. Examples include:

◊ Thank you letters from students

◊ A simple plaque or certificate of appreciation that can be hung in the business partner's office

◊ A celebration/recognition breakfast or luncheon

◊ A press release to the local newspaper

◊ A newsletter item that can be included in the business partner's internal newspaper

◊ A letter of appreciation to the business partner's boss or supervisor

A recognition item doesn't have to be expensive. But celebrating even a small "win" is always a big deal for the volunteer. Regularly recognizing and celebrating wins serves to keep your board members energized and refreshed.

Overcoming Advisory Board Realities and Challenges

CTE programs, and their advisory boards, can face common or uncommon challenges over time. Here are a few of the ones you may face, and how you can address them.

Business partner complacency, apathy, or fear

Prospective business partners may be reluctant to get involved for a variety of reasons:

- Ignorance – "How could one business person possibly make a difference?"
- Complacency – "It was good enough for me when I was in high school."
- Apathy – "It's not my problem, besides, I'm too busy."
- Fear – "I haven't been in a high school since I graduated."
- Misconceptions – "It's just glorified baby-sitting; there isn't any real learning going on in there."
- Media Hype – "Our high schools are full of drugs, gangs, teen pregnancies and shootings."

Overcoming these barriers is part of the role of the advisory board recruitment committee members. These business partners understand the role of the business partner and the benefits that can inure to the business partner, both professional and personally, as well as to their company, from being involved with your program. Delegate board recruiting to the partners who can "talk the talk" and "walk the walk".

School/district restructure

A change in the programming or philosophy of a school or district may inadvertently torpedo a very successful program, "throwing out the baby with the bathwater." To avoid this, or at least minimize this risk, program leaders should ask their advisory board members to speak with the principal, superintendent, school board, parents, chamber of commerce education committee, etc. to preserve a successful program in a school, despite any changes at the school or district level.

Superintendent/principal turnover

As "captains" of the school district or school building, the Superintendent and/or the Principal often have the last word when it comes to deciding which programs are incorporated into the curriculum, and which are not. Sadly, excellent programs are sometimes closed when a superintendent or principal changes. Your advisory board members can be a very strong, supportive voice for you and your program, if there is a threat that your program will close or you will lose your funding.

Program leader change

If a program leader/director is lost, it may signal the end of the program. A strong school-based leader with a passion for the program is often difficult to replace, resulting in a decline in the efficacy, size, or functionality of the program. This issue should be planned for, even if there are no immediate changes on the horizon, in the event a program leader is transferred to a new school, reassigned to a different department, or otherwise changes roles in a school.

Business partners transfer, are promoted, or leave

Business is an ever-changing environment for your partners. In order to continue to be successful, your business partners may be required to change jobs within their company; change venues, territories, or offices; move locations; assume new, different and more challenging responsibilities, etc. As a result, you may lose valuable business partners from your program. To help overcome this problem, consider the following:

- Make advisory board recruiting an ongoing practice; add a "board recruitment" committee to your board
- Provide guidelines in your by-laws for business partner replacement/succession
- Encourage exiting partners to "fill their own vacancy" with a suitable representative from their company
- In very special cases, consider "remote" involvement from partners who can no longer regularly attend meetings face to face

Funding reduced or lost

Program success often relies on funding from the district, the state, the federal government, etc. If/when this funding is reduced or lost, the program can be seriously jeopardized. Sometimes, your advisory board members' companies can help to make up shortfalls in funding. Also, funding can come from the Fundraising Committee of your advisory boards. And finally, your board members can assist in advocating on behalf of your program to your principal, superintendent, school board and/or state department of education to keep the program funds flowing, despite overall budget cuts.

EET Case Studies

About These Case Studies

The case studies in this section are designed to illustrate many of the different ways that schools can work with their business partners, showcasing real-world applications of the partnership models outlined in Section II. You may find a model that fits your needs exactly; if not, these files will at least give you a practical feel for how partnerships are set up and how they operate.

The case files in this section include:

◊ Door County Career Awareness Campaign

◊ Luxottica Mentoring Partnership

◊ Operation Excellence

◊ Principal/Business Mentor Program

◊ Gowan Achievement Project

◊ Pacific Life Foundation's Nonprofit Internship Experience

◊ LEAD Program

◊ NJ Chamber of Commerce Foundation

◊ Unum's "Tech Night" Program

◊ Teachers Warehouse

◊ Houston A+ Challenge Teacher Externships

◊ WorkReady Philadelphia

◊ Florida PASS Program

◊ Calgary's Career Pathways Initiative

◊ Rockwell Collins' Engineering Experiences

Door County Career Awareness Campaign

In many high schools, a "college for all" approach prevents many students from learning about the full array of career opportunities open to them. In Door County, Wisconsin, pressing workforce needs provided business leaders with an incentive to overcome that challenge, and led them to build a career awareness program with their local schools.

According to Tara LeClair, manager of the Business and Education Partnership for the Door County Economic Development Corporation (EDC), there's an unfortunate fact about the students coming out of local high schools: "Once they graduate, they leave," she says. "And they don't come back." This has created a workforce shortage in this area, particularly in manufacturing and healthcare – the county's largest industries.

The EDC started working closely with its business members to address the shortage in available workers, a situation made more pronounced since many in the current manufacturing workforce are of retirement age and beginning to leave. Without an increase in the number of local qualified workers, businesses are left with two options: bring workers in from other locations, or close shop and open where workers are available.

The EDC took this issue to the local schools so they could work together on a solution, and one idea from those sessions was particularly appealing: why not showcase the careers available with local employers and share that information with every high school student in the district?

Career tech directors agreed that there was a need to expose students to careers in manufacturing, but noted that they had not had much success to date: the materials they had available to them, particularly videos highlighting various careers, were of poor quality. These videos were generic, they were old (20 years old or more), and they portrayed manufacturing in an unflattering light, featuring dark and dirty work environments and low-skill jobs.

EDC staff and their business partners knew they could do better. They recognized that manufacturing positions with local companies are found in clean, professional facilities, and that the work, in addition to being high-paying, was interesting, challenging, involved the use of advanced technology, and offered opportunities for advancement. They had a story they could tell; the question now was how to tell it.

The partners realized that they needed to let students see the reality of the manufacturing opportunities with local employers, and decided to create their own multimedia content, complete with actual employees talking about the work they did and showing them in real local work environments.

The Career Awareness Campaign

Where:
Door County, WI

Partner(s):
Door County EDC; local manufacturers; several local school districts (including superintendents who sit on the board of the business/education partnership)

Challenge:
High school students not aware of opportunities with local companies and moving out of the area after graduation; local employers not finding employees, either bringing in workers from elsewhere or closing down and moving

Solution:
Develop a series of career videos featuring opportunities found with local employers. Film employees talking about their jobs and operating within an actual work environment and provide basic information, such as education required and compensation. Distribute to every high school student in the area (multiple districts) through principals, as well as to students in technical colleges and others

Partner Roles:
Business partners helped fund the video series, helped to identify the careers to be highlighted, and provided employees to be featured. School and district partners ensure widespread distribution by sending emails through internal channels

Outcomes:
While still early, employers have received positive feedback and are already starting to see job applicants for positions featured in the series

After receiving support through a grant request to a local foundation, and with business partners covering remaining costs, they moved ahead.

The EDC's business partners produced a series of brief videos, each featuring a different manufacturing career, and each hosted at a different employer's location. They felt it was important to use a young, often recently graduated, employee – someone students could relate to, or may even know – and they took the time to ensure that those employees became comfortable on camera so that they would present a relaxed, professional demeanor.

The partners contracted the video production work

Below: an example of the career awareness emails sent out to high school students in Door County, WI by the Door County EDC's Business and Education Partnership.

to a company in nearby Green Bay called WebOuts, which offered a special technology that produced engaging online video. Not only was the technology naturally high-interest, but the prospect of online distribution was appealing: the partners felt that DVDs, in addition to being far more expensive and logistically challenging, would be less likely to be used by students.

Working with the partnership, WebOuts created a series of nine brief videos, each focused on a different career. Students clicking into one of the videos are greeted with an introduction from a local employee, who talks briefly about his or her career of choice and invites the student to view the selected video. The video contains more information on the career in question along with footage of the employee at the workplace. Each email and video list participating business partners at the bottom; students can click through to learn about career opportunities with these local employers.

Because the superintendents of seven local school districts sit on the board of the business and education partnership and were involved in the planning of this project, the EDC was able to send emails to every high school student at local schools – not just those already involved in CTE classes. A total of nine emails were sent, one per month, and each featuring a different career. Principals of local schools were responsible for sending the emails, which allowed the partnership to avoid list collection and management; this also allowed the emails to come through internal channels, and not look as if they came from an outside group.

Beyond high school distribution, the EDC distributes the videos through contacts with area technical colleges and maintains a distribution list

Resource Links

Door County EDC
www.doorcountybusiness.com

Door County EDC Career Videos
www.doorcountybusiness.com/WebOuts/EWebOuts/CNCMachining_EWO2.html

WebOuts LLC
www.webouts.com

that includes the press, local business leaders, and others. This supplemental distribution increases the impact and exposure of the project.

The partnership developed this project with an eye towards the workforce pipeline; according to LeClair, the project's core audience is found in the early high school grades, and the businesses asked to participate are those who anticipate having job opportunities within the next three to five years – just when those 9th and 10th graders will be graduating and looking for work.

While this project is still not through its first year of implementation, early returns have been encouraging: manufacturers are getting positive feedback from the campaign, and some are already beginning to see job inquiries directly attributable to the program. If response continues to be strong, the project partners have indicated an interest in producing a second round of videos, spotlighting additional careers and employers.

And as this project progresses, the Door County EDC stays busy with two career preparedness programs: one focused on the construction trades, in which students build a house each year, which is then sold to help fund the program; and the other focused on preparing students for careers as medical technicians. This trio of programs, all created and managed with the support of district leaders and other partnership board members, are making an appreciable difference in meeting workforce needs in their community.

Luxottica Mentoring Partnership

While there are many ways in which community members can impact the life of a child, mentoring stands out as one of the most powerful, popular, and heavily researched models available. Luxottica Retail, guided by the expertise of the Cincinnati Youth Collaborative, has established a corporate initiative that utilizes the power of long-term mentoring to produce dramatic changes in the lives of students at a local high school as well as the lives of the mentors who work with them.

Origin of the mentoring partnership

With North American headquarters in Cincinnati, Milan-based Luxottica is the world's leading designer, manufacturer, and distributor of premium and luxury prescription frames and sunglasses. The company is best known for retail brands, including LensCrafters, Pearle Vision, and Sunglass Hut, as well as for eyewear brands including Oakley, Ray-Ban, and many others.

Luxottica has a history of community involvement. According to Keith Borders, VP of Associate Relations, Diversity, and HR Compliance, "Luxottica has a culture of inclusion and giving back; we believe that a company can and should be profitable while sharing its business expertise and talents to make a positive difference in our local communities and around the world."

In 2001, this commitment to inclusion and social engagement led the company's Diversity Community Committee, made up of employees, to look for ways to reach out to underserved youth in Cincinnati. After considering their options, they honed in on mentoring as a way for employees to share their time and talents over an extended period in order to make the greatest possible impact on participating youth.

They were fortunate to find a local organization with expertise in mentoring: the Cincinnati Youth Collaborative (CYC), a nonprofit founded by members of the Cincinnati community in 1987. The group was created to try to reduce the rising failure and dropout rates in the Cincinnati Public Schools and to help every youth in Cincinnati realize his or her potential. CYC's dual focus on mentoring and college access were a perfect match with Luxottica's interests, and they collaborated on the creation of the company's new initiative.

Structure of the program

Working with CYC, members of the Diversity Community Committee designed a workplace mentoring program intended to support and inspire students to graduate from high school and go to college. The program was structured so that company employees, both mentors and others, could interact with students in a professional

Luxottica Mentoring Partnership

Where:
Cincinnati, OH

Partner(s):
The Diversity Community Committee of Luxottica Retail (headquarters location), Cincinnati Youth Collaborative (CYC), Cincinnati Public Schools

Challenge:
Help improve outcomes for local underserved students, with an emphasis on graduating high school and exploring and pursuing post-secondary opportunities

Solution:
Develop a long-term mentoring initiative to focus on academic, social, and professional development, matching students from a local high school with Luxottica employees. Monthly mentoring sessions take place at the company's headquarters, and focus on mentoring, relationship development, and skill-building ranging from public speaking to completing college and grant applications. Special events may involve community service or visiting local college campuses. The company now offers a number of scholarships to graduating participants.

Partner Roles:
Luxottica's Diversity Community Committee designs and implements the program, with CYC supporting their work through training and consulting.

Outcomes:
More than 100 students have been involved in the program; 97% have graduated high school. One hundred percent of last year's graduating students went on to college.

environment, helping students connect their school experiences with the world of work. The program was intended to help students explore career interests, prepare for and pursue post-secondary options, and build strong, possibly life-long, relationships with caring adults.

As they developed this initiative, committee members set an overarching partnership goal, which is to assist students, including many low income and first generation, to reach their full potential by focusing on education and building life skills. They set four specific project goals, including:

◊ Assist students in graduating from high school

◊ Assist students in preparing for post-secondary options

◊ Assist students in enrolling in post-secondary education

◊ Assist students in building community awareness by involving them in the community

To achieve these goals, committee members created a model in which students from a partner high school would visit the company's headquarters on a monthly basis to spend time with their mentor in a professional environment. They chose nearby Withrow High School as their partner school based on its proximity and its focus on post-secondary attainment.

The program maintains a long-term focus, with students and mentors being matched at the start of the 9th grade and continuing their relationships throughout the high school years. There are 50 such relationships at any one time, ninth graders joining each year after a comparable number of seniors have graduated.

As the program developed, Luxottica and CYC continued to improve its design and operation. Characteristics of the program include:

◊ Partners consider logistical issues in all their plans, and work to ensure that space, training, transportation, funding, and time away from school do not become obstacles for the program.

◊ Each monthly session combines mentoring and skill development: mentors and mentees share lunch and conversation, and then participate in a planned activity ranging from attending public speaking classes to filling out college and scholarship applications. Students learn practical skills from professional role models who share similar interests and cultural/ethnic backgrounds.

◊ Luxottica has designed a back-up mentor program so every student always has a mentor available, even when the primary mentor is traveling.

◊ In addition to the monthly meetings, Luxottica involves students in other dimensions of the company's culture of giving back to the local community. For example, students participate in Luxottica's Hometown Days, a week of hands-on service during which Luxottica associates provide free eye exams and vision care.

◊ Each year, Luxottica establishes a program theme with customized activities that include college visits, career exploration and "Earn to Learn" assignments that allow students to earn points throughout the year towards prizes.

◊ The company has begun offering scholarships, $4,000 each spread out over four years, which are awarded at the end of the program. Students compete for the scholarships by making presentations to a panel of committee members and executives.

Keith Borders of Luxottica, speaking from personal experience as one of the program's mentors, notes that "while the program is focused on workplace skills, we also emphasize academic and social skills. I make a point to involve my mentee in family

Resource Links

Luxottica Retail
www.luxottica.com/english/index.html

Cincinnati Youth Collaborative
www.cycyouth.org

activities, whether we're having fun or doing something like paying the bills. It's important for him to see how people live independently and responsibly."

Partnership Roles

The design and operation of the program has been collaborative: CYC provides support in the form of training, consulting, and expertise, and Luxottica employees lead on design and implementation. The school district, and Withrow administrators and teachers in particular, have been highly supportive in promoting the program and ensuring that students can participate.

Budget

Funding for the program has grown with its success. The initial annual budget was $6,800 and has grown to $14,300 including lunch expenses, supplies, transportation, and two $4,000 college scholarships. Two additional scholarships have just been added to the program. Volunteer hours are valued at $51,700 and CYC provides coordinating support for the program.

Outcomes

According to Jane Keller, CYC executive director, over 100 students have been involved in the program to date: 97% of those students graduated high school, and 100% of last year's seniors have gone on to college. While the program initially solicited recommendations for students to participate, Keller notes that "the program now runs on word of mouth - students throughout the school are aware of it and want to get involved." And Borders notes that mentors report a great enthusiasm for the initiative, which translates into morale and retention, two areas important to the company.

Campaign leaders at Luxottica and CYC note that they are focused on continually improving the program; since its founding, the partners have enhanced training, measurement, program features, and outreach to the corporate community (Luxottica has shared its best practices with organizations such as General Electric Aviation and Procter and Gamble). This program will certainly continue to develop as it extends into the future.

Operation Excellence

The majority of business/education partnerships focus on improving student outcomes through direct or indirect engagement at the classroom or individual student level. However, there are other opportunities for engaging the business community, and for those willing to think outside the classroom, the rewards can be quite remarkable.

One example comes from the Montgomery County Business Roundtable for Education (MCBRE), a nonprofit operating in Montgomery County, Maryland (north of Washington DC). One of the organization's first community/school initiatives, Operation Excellence, is an example of a nontraditional partnership model that fully leveraged the time and talents of business partners and had a dramatic influence on school, and ultimately student, outcomes.

The origin of Operation Excellence

When Dr. Jerry Weast joined Montgomery County Public Schools (MCPS) as Superintendent in 1999, he brought with him a firm belief in the value of building strong relationships with the business community. He had seen the impact of such relationships in previous districts and immediately began reaching out to local business leaders upon his arrival in Montgomery County.

Dr. Weast was one of the local leaders who brought about the creation of MCBRE in 2000. The organization was founded, and continues to operate, as a bridge for the creation of strategic business/education partnerships, focusing on connecting classroom learning to the workplace and on improving the quality of school operations. The organization emphasizes communication and collaboration between the district and the business community: Dr. Weast sits on the board, and district officials are involved in the design and planning of major initiatives.

Within two years of the organization's founding, Michael Subin, President of the Montgomery County Council, asked the Executive Director of

MCBRE to coordinate a study of targeted business operations of the district. The goal of the project, according to the Operation Excellence summary report, was "to use business acumen to identify ways of making some of the MCPS business processes more efficient and effective with the idea of re-allocating the savings to the instructional programs of MCPS, which directly benefit the children of the county."

While district leaders in some areas would be wary of such an initiative, MCPS leaders embraced the opportunity due in part to three factors:

Operation Excellence

Where:
Montgomery County, Maryland

Partner(s):
Montgomery County Business Roundtable for Education; Montgomery County Public Schools; multiple individuals representing various businesses

Challenge:
Find efficiencies in district operations so that funds freed up could enhance instructional efforts

Solution:
MCBRE, working with representatives of MCPS and the local business community, targeted four operational areas and put together a team to study each one and provide suggestions for improvement.

Partner Roles:
Two community leaders, Jane Rudolph with Lockheed Martin and Larry Bowers with MCPS, led the project, identifying areas of study and working with MCBRE staff to recruit and manage partners for each team. Team members worked together for three months to analyze existing operations and make recommendations.

Outcomes:
The district realized several direct and indirect outcomes. They were able to rethink strategic approaches to building maintenance and cleaning and lobby for new equipment, all of which significantly reduced hiring needs in those areas. Further, acquisition of software in call center and financial operations areas improved capabilities in those areas.

Indirectly, several of the business partners continued their support for the district after the project ended, and many gained knowledge they could apply to their own work. The district, through this and other community engagement efforts, continues to build support throughout the county.

◊ The Superintendent placed a high priority on community engagement, particularly on bringing the business community into school operations as true partners.

◊ The project was proposed in order to increase resources flowing into instruction, not simply to reduce budgets overall.

◊ While MCBRE was a new organization, school and community leaders had worked on a similar initiative in 1993 called the Corporate Partnership for Managerial Excellence (CPME). The majority of the recommendations of CPME had been implemented and all parties viewed it as a success.

Project design and implementation

MCBRE selected two people to structure and lead the initiative. The first was a representative of the business community who sat on MCBRE's Board: Jane Rudolph, Vice President of Strategic Analysis and Development for Lockheed Martin. The second was Larry Bowers, Chief Operating Officer for MCPS.

Working together over the course of several weeks, these project leaders identified four operational areas to review, based in part on Bowers' analysis of where improvements could be made and efficiencies found. These included:

◊ Facilities management

◊ Financial management

◊ Technology management

◊ Baldrige certification

According to Larry Bowers, "This was a partnership that allowed businesspeople to share their expertise on the operations side of the shop. It can be difficult to involve people on the education side because for some it's not their background, but when it comes to business operations, they're extremely familiar and have a great deal to offer."

Once they had identified these target areas, Rudolph and Bowers, with the help of MCBRE staff, put together a set of strategic questions for each area, a step that helped guide their selection of

business partners. Altogether, Operation Excellence recruited 25 business leaders and 13 district leaders to fulfill the goals of the project.

MCBRE recruited people based on their individual expertise, regardless of whether their companies focused primarily in the target area in question. As Jane Rudolph notes, "Lockheed Martin supported the team with people out of our financial community to help look at their financial systems. That's not normally what you would think about Lockheed Martin doing, but as we saw where their needs were, we looked across our organization to see how we could contribute to the effort. Clearly, we work with large-scale financial systems here, and we wanted to bring that experience and expertise to look at their systems to see what they might need to make them more efficient."

Once teams were assembled in each focus area, those teams were given three months to analyze current operations, review options, and make recommendations. Each team established their own structure, workflow, and meeting schedule. A kickoff was held at the County Office Building on June 18, 2003 and the results were submitted to MCBRE by the business leaders on or around September 25, 2003. The final recommendations document was made public in October of 2003 in a presentation to the Montgomery County Council.

Direct outcomes of Operation Excellence

After MCPS and the County Council reviewed the partners' recommendations, they decided to put several into place; this include allocating funds from the council for needed software and equipment. Some examples highlighted by Larry Bowers include:

◊ The partners found that the district's financial management software, first purchased in 1983, was incapable of meeting current needs. They identified a new system with the necessary features, and the business partners successfully lobbied the County Council for the funding. "Businesspeople are influential advocates," said Bowers. "Elected officials look to business leaders for input."

- ◊ Business partners also lobbied for the purchase of equipment that allowed the district to forgo the hiring of additional building services staff.

- ◊ The partners established a different strategic approach to cleaning, going from a model with one person handling all duties within an area to a team model that moved through a facility together.

- ◊ Maintenance staff are deployed differently as a result of the team's recommendations. They have significantly reduced staff time on the road by having staff handle multiple work orders with each site visit, going to the extent of cross-training some staff members to increase their capabilities. Materials delivery models were also restructured.

- ◊ Call center operations, particularly those in the district's employees and retiree services office, were improved as well. United Healthcare was particularly helpful in giving team members a tour of their call center facility, walking them through UHC operations, helping the district choose and purchase call center software, and helping set up a center within the district office.

As a result of these and other improvements, the district has not hired any additional maintenance staff since 2003, despite adding six million square feet of facility space. (Additional staff have been hired in building services, but not at all in proportion to this growth.)

Indirect outcomes

In addition to the cost savings and improvements made possible as a direct result of this campaign, the district has realized several indirect outcomes.

First, many of the business partners involved in Operation Excellence have continued to support the district and to advocate on its behalf. This has been helpful in ongoing improvement efforts and, more broadly, in advocating for the district with the County Council and others.

While the school district was intended as the

beneficiary of this project, many of the participating businesspeople reported learning a great deal through the process as well, particularly in areas such as the implementation of Six Sigma programs (used by MCPS as part of its Baldrige efforts).

Also, according to Jane Rudolph, "One thing we learned through this process is that, in a number of areas, MCPS is doing a fabulous job - there were really no efficiencies to be gained. It's good to have that kind of information about a public institution - it instills confidence on the part of businesses and others in the community."

Due in part to the openness of the district to this effort, and the respect it earned from its business partners, MCPS continues to garner support and strengthen its reputation within the community. According to Larry Bowers, the district has seen a net increase of 6,000 students coming from private institutions over the last eight years, and its market share has increased from 80% to 84% of school-aged children in that time. And the collaborative approach the parties brought to Operation Excellence has helped MCBRE and MCPS build a strong and trusting working relationship that has allowed for additional successes over the years.

While business/education partnerships that call upon the professional expertise of the business community may not be common, the work of those involved in Operation Excellence shows that they can have a dramatic effect on district operations and on stakeholder relations. As district leaders work to address the challenges presented by today's economic climate, they should consider the benefits of such initiatives and approach their business partners accordingly.

Resource Links

Montgomery County Business Roundtable for Education
www.mcbre.org

Operation Excellence Recommendations Report
www.mcbre.org/Library/OperationExcellenceResultsFinal.pdf

Montgomery County Public Schools
www.montgomeryschoolsmd.org

Corporate Partnership for Managerial Excellence Report
The 1993 predecessor to Operation Excellence
www.quality.org/tqmbbs/govt/cpme.txt

The Principal/Business Mentor Program

Student mentoring is a common activity among business/education partnerships, and there is a great deal of evidence to support its effectiveness in boosting student outcomes. Less common - but no less effective - are mentoring programs that pair business leaders with teachers and/or administrators. After setting up just such a program in 2007, Partners in Education of Toledo, a standalone partnership organization, has seen positive results for its efforts.

History

Partners In Education of Toledo (PIE) was founded in 1994 by the Rotary Club of Toledo, with support from the Toledo Area Chamber of Commerce, area banks and corporations. While members of the Rotary Club had been actively volunteering in local schools for some time, they decided to create PIE in order to create a pathway for others to be more easily connected to the schools, and in the early years PIE focused primarily on establishing and promoting volunteering and mentoring opportunities for members of the community, and has also launched scholarship and internship programs along with a Principal for the Day initiative. Now in its 15th year, it is now funded and supported by a wide base of businesses, individuals, and other community entities.

In 2007, based on the organization's success in supporting area schools, superintendent John Foley of the Toledo Public Schools asked PIE to explore the idea of a mentoring program for new middle and high school principals. According to Foley, those coming into a leadership position for the first time may have experience in the field (most new administrators are former teachers), but they may not have experience or training in management, leadership, operations, or other areas that are critical to their success. Business leaders who had led successful companies, he reasoned, may be able to mentor these new principals and help them quickly gain the knowledge and skills they needed to succeed across all areas.

After an initial pilot program to test the concept and establish a base program design, PIE committed to launching the Principal/Business Mentoring Program as one of their core initiatives. This coincided with the arrival of Eileen Kerner as executive director, who has overseen the development and expansion of the program following its pilot phase.

Program Design

The Principal/Business Mentoring Program is a joint effort of PIE, Toledo Association of Administrative Personnel, Toledo Public Schools, and Toledo Regional Chamber of Commerce. The program focuses on matching a local business leader with

Principal/Business Mentor Program

Where:
Toledo, OH

Partner(s):
Partners in Education of Toledo, Toledo Association of Administrative Personnel, Toledo Regional Chamber of Commerce, Toledo Public Schools, local business leaders, Toledo Federation of Teachers

Challenge:
First-time principals of middle and high schools face challenges in multiple areas, including not only academics but also personnel, administration, and operations - there is a need to help these new administrators continue to develop their management skills

Solution:
Match area business leaders with new principals in a mentoring role, supporting these new relationships with workshops and ongoing contacts; the program recently added a teacher union representative to each building-level relationship to increase buy-in on the part of educators

Partner Roles:
Business leaders and principals in a mentor/mentee role work together to set and achieve specific managerial and organizational goals, with significant support from PIE

Outcomes:
Because every mentoring relationship sets its own unique objectives, there is not a single metric being tracked to gauge outcomes among schools; however, post-program surveys given to business and school leaders show great enthusiasm for the program, and PIE has heard multiple anecdotal success stories.

a new principal in the Toledo Public Schools. The principal must be new, and he or she must be in a middle or high school, since administrators in those schools often face greater challenges (ranging from school size to student behavior) than principals of elementary schools. The program runs over an approximate six month period, taking place in the winter and spring seasons.

The business leader does not have to be a CEO, but must have built a track record in his or her career and must have proven leadership and management skills. Many, but not all, of these businesspeople come to the program through PIE's other programs, and are looking for other ways to contribute to local schools; Kerner has also made a concerted effort to reach out to new business partners to encourage participation in this program. She finds a great deal of support for this and other programs from the business community: many of these individuals grew up locally and attended these schools, and feel a real desire to give something back, and they realize that by helping one principal to become more effective, they can impact the lives of literally thousands of children over time.

The mentoring program includes two key elements: individual relationships, established and guided by the decisions of each mentor/mentee pair; and a series of formal learning opportunities allowing each set of partners to learn about change management.

Individual relationships
The core of this program, like any other mentoring initiative, lies in the individual relationships established between the mentor and the mentee. Once principals and business leaders have been assigned to one another, they are encouraged to set an introductory meeting on the school grounds prior to any formal events or meetings (as outlined below). While many of the business partners have had some exposure to the schools through other PIE initiatives, the challenges faced by each individual school are different, and more importantly, the strengths and priorities of each new principal vary and must be considered when laying out the direction of the mentoring relationship.

Partners are encouraged to start by talking about the circumstances at the school, and deciding together what should be their objectives for the mentoring term. This may relate to developing management or leadership skills in the principal, launching a program to address some specific issue, or something else. But partners are encouraged to set some kind of goal and work towards it throughout the term of the program.

One the relationship has been established and goals have been set (or are at least in the process of being set), mentors and mentees are expected to meet at least once per month to talk and progress toward their goals; this is in addition to participating in the formal learning opportunities. Additional contact is encouraged, and many partners find regular contact by telephone and email to be helpful.

Formal training
PIE has developed a relationship with Dr. Clinton Longenecker, a nationally recognized leader in the field of rapid performance improvement and a professor in the College of Business Administration at the University of Toledo. Dr. Longenecker, author of *Two Minute Drill: Lessons for Rapid Organizational Improvement from America's Greatest Game*, conducts a series of hands-on workshops for program participants that are based on lessons from this book and from his other work (see sidebar at right for a description of sessions for 2010).

In addition to attending these workshops, program participants are encouraged to read *Two Minute Drill* and incorporate these ideas into their efforts throughout the course of the program.

This year's program saw a significant enhancement: inviting a representative of the Toledo Federation of Teachers (TFT) to participate in the mentoring program at each school. This provided teachers at the building with a voice into the goals and processes of the project at the building level, and correspondingly allowed for greater buy-in from educators at each school. PIE saw strong participation from these educator representatives and expect to see this element continue into the future.

PIE's Experience with the Program

Any partnership operation must look at the ROI of its programs: what it invests in its initiatives versus what outcomes it produces. For PIE, this program has proven to be a very strong investment. It has low financial requirements: most of the investment comes in the time spent recruiting businesspeople and developing training opportunities, supplemented with time spent monitoring the progress of individual relationships and being on call for questions or support. There is a financial investment in terms of setting up the training sessions (renting space, providing food, etc.), but all in all the program carries a relatively low total cost, enjoys significant support from the community and the schools, and produces positive outcomes for the schools and the district.

Outcomes

While the program cannot track universal outcomes - each pair sets and achieves different goals based on their needs - they have clearly seen signs of success in the post-program surveys completed by the participants. Participants have all said the program was valuable, a good investment of their time, and resulted in real and desired outcomes for the principal and the school. In addition, PIE notes that many of the mentor/mentee relationships have continued beyond the program year.

With a relatively low investment and solid outcomes, this program shows that mentoring programs do not have to be limited to students - administrators (and teachers) can realize great benefits from partners in their communities.

Resource Links

Partners in Education of Toledo
www.partnerstoledo.org

The Two Minute Drill
www.amazon.com/Two-Minute-Drill-Organizational-Improvement/dp/0787994901

Program Description/Meeting Agenda for Mentoring Series
from Partners in Education of Toledo

The Principal/Business Mentor Program is supported by a series of learning sessions led by Dr. Clint Longenecker, Stranahan Professor of Leadership and Organizational Excellence at the University of Toledo, and author of *Two Minute Drill: Lessons for Rapid Organizational Improvement from America's Greatest Game*. These sessions bring together program participants to learn about and work through key issues related to organizational improvement. Topics for the 2010 series included the following:

Understanding the Real Dynamics of Change/Improvement
Thursday, February 4; 4-5:30 pm
- Why change efforts fail and succeed
- A review of various processes improvement models

The Critical Role of Leadership in the Change Process
Thursday, February 18; 4-5:30 pm
- The practices of effective change quarterbacks/leaders
- Developing your capacity for leading and executing change

A Two-Minute Drill Model to Rapid Performance Improvement
Thursday, March 18; 4-5:30 pm
- Developing a comprehensive understanding of successful rapid performance improvement
- How to apply TMD thinking and executing to your current approach to change

How to Run a Two-Minute Drill in Your Organization
Thursday, April 15; 4-5:30 pm
- Selecting your opportunity to implement a rapid performance improvement initiative
- Developing your game plan to execute your TMD

Excerpts from the Program Description:
Better performance always requires change and organizations are using a wide variety of process improvement tools to achieve this goal. If you are like most managers, your most important resource is time, so speed and execution in the improvement process are the name of the game. This development program will explore how leaders approach the process of change and guide them through a systematic analysis of how to accelerate real and rapid performance improvement.

Managers will explore their role as "quarterbacks" in the change process. Participants will learn how to create a sense of urgency and importance around their next improvement initiative and how to conduct an effective scouting report on their opponents that they will face in their change efforts. Managers will learn the principles of managing the clock, executing each and every play in their improvement plan, using scoreboards to track progress, the importance of building momentum into their improvement efforts, and ensuring that change delivers tangible outcomes (and not just activity). Finally, the transformational experience will help leaders come to the realization that celebrating success and conducting post-change analyses is paramount to creating a culture conducive to rapid organizational improvement.

The Gowan Achievement Project

When people talk about workforce issues and K12 education, they're usually talking about preparing kids for employment opportunities after high school. But there are other ways in which the two intersect: for example, the reputation of local schools can be a significant factor for employees with children who are being asked to transfer into a new market.

This had become an issue for the Gowan Company, which provides crop protection products and services to farmers and others. While it has offices around the world, the company's headquarters are in Yuma, Arizona, where it employs more than 500 people. Gowan relies heavily on a scientific workforce, and often hires people from other parts of the country for positions at its headquarters. However, because of a perception that local schools could not adequately meet the needs of advanced students, the company has faced challenges in attracting workers with children to the area.

Jon Jessen, founder and president of this family-owned company, decided to approach the Crane School District directly so they could address this issue together. Jessen was no stranger to the local district: he had previously served on the Crane Governing Board (the local school board); Caroline, his wife, had taught at a local elementary school; and all four of his children had attended Crane Schools. Gowan and the Jessen family also have a long history of investing time and resources into Yuma's youth through college scholarships and other investments.

Jessen discussed his concerns with Cindy Baker, who is one of Gowan's presidents as well as a member of the Crane Governing Board. She initiated a conversation with Cindy Didway, Crane's superintendent, and they quickly put together a strategy and planning team made up of internal and external leaders.

The project

The team started by taking a look at the facts, and

realized that there may be some truth to the idea that the school district was not meeting the needs of advanced students. Like other districts around the country, Crane was responsible for bringing all children to grade level, and this priority, combined with limited resources, meant that students already performing at or above grade level may not have access to all the opportunities the district would like.

Working from that reality, Gowan and Crane decided to create an initiative open exclusively to students already performing at or above grade

---

The Gowan Achievement Project

Where:
Crane School District, Yuma, Arizona

Partner(s):
Gowan Company, which offers crop protection products and services, with offices around the world and 500 employees in the Yuma area

Challenge:
Gowan Company had a difficult time recruiting employees to the area - a perception existed that schools were focused on bringing underperforming students to grade level, not meeting the needs of students at or above grade level. Gowan also wanted to ensure the preparedness of the local workforce in the future.

Solution:
The Gowan Achievement Project piloted with 90 children in grades 4, 5, and 6 who were performing at or above grade level. Children were placed in classes with master teachers, given laptops with wifi access, experienced a math- and science-intensive curriculum, and participated in special activities such as field trips that emphasize STEM careers and industries.

Partner Roles:
Gowan underwrote the pilot, including the cost of all technology and $10,000 grants for master teachers; it also helped design the program, participated in the hiring of the master teachers, has representatives on an advisory board, and participates in the program through classroom visits and field trips. Crane manages operation of the program.

Outcomes:
A test/control model was established to evaluate impact. GAP students outperformed their peers in math by 2:1 in Average Percent Gain Per Student, and by 8:1 in science. AIMS scores for 4th grade science show 93% proficiency for GAP students versus a statewide average of 53%.

---

level; furthermore, given Gowan's need for a future workforce with science and math skills, and the interests of its transferring employees, the partners decided to emphasize math and science through its initiative.

Starting from this point, the partners created The Gowan Achievement Project according to the following parameters:

◊ **Grade levels** - GAP focused the project in the upper elementary grades (4, 5, 6); Crane is a K-8 district, and focusing on grades 4-6 allowed them to work with children who had been identified in grade 3 as performing at or above grade level through independent measures.

◊ **Pilot site** - The team decided to pilot the program at Rancho Viejo Elementary School, which has the highest free/reduced lunch rate (a commonly used indicator of poverty) in the district. If the pilot succeeded there, they felt confident that GAP would be successful elsewhere.

◊ **Instruction** - To ensure that participating students were challenged through a range of experiences, the partners decided to bring in master teachers to lead the pilot classes. The positions were posted within the district, and prospective teachers interviewed with the planning team and were asked to teach a quick lesson. The district picked up the cost of the positions, but Gowan supplied a $10,000 stipend for each of them.

◊ **Technology** - The partners felt it was important to promote technological literacy, and designed GAP accordingly. Each participating student received a laptop computer; wireless access was set up in each classroom; and students had access to a variety of peripherals (digital cameras, projectors, etc.) for use in classroom projects.

◊ **Science/math** - Given Gowan's interests, and those of its transferring employees, the project was designed with a strong foundation in science and math. Crane

selected an electronic curriculum called A+ K12 Learning Courseware, which met their requirements for networking purposes, pre-testing, curriculum variety, and ease of use. Teachers received training in the use of the curriculum.

◊ **Rich learning experiences** - Students participated in field trips reinforcing science and math concepts and focused on career and college preparedness. These included trips to the Arizona Science Center, Lake Powell, local state universities, and Gowan Company headquarters. Additionally, students produced multimedia presentations and research papers on these visits and on topics related to the environment, geology, ecology, and Native American history and culture.

◊ **Oversight** - Individuals on the strategic planning team formed an advisory committee to review the progress of the program during quarterly meetings and to determine next steps for the program.

◊ **Evaluation** - To determine the impact of GAP, students participated in pre- and post-assessments in all areas of the curriculum; the district also set up a control group at another school and tracked their progress on key metrics. GAP student performance was also compared to statewide averages.

As initiator of the project and sole corporate partner, The Gowan Company took an active role in designing, funding, and overseeing the project. They also were heavily involved in discussions about the level and role that technology would play in the project; participated in interviews of prospective master teachers as part of their advisory committee role; and hosted students at their corporate headquarters on a field trip. And based on the success of the project to date, they have also been instrumental in planning for the future - including covering the costs of a rollout to other sites within the district.

Results to date

As noted previously, GAP project leaders

performed pre/post evaluations with participating students, and set up a control group at a different school comprised of students academically and socioeconomically similar to those in the pilot. Outcomes from the one-year pilot include:

◊ GAP students outperformed their counterparts in every areas in which the electronic curriculum was utilized.

◊ In the area of 4th-6th grade math, GAP students outpaced the control group by two to one in the Average Percent Gain Per Student.

◊ In 4th-6th grade combined science scores, GAP students stretched that growth to eight times the Average Percent Gain Per Student against the control group.

◊ In 4th grade science, the average for the statewide assessment (AIMS) was 53%; for GAP students, it was 93%.

◊ Two 5th grade GAP students each won 2nd place ribbons at the Yuma County Science Fair, the first time Rancho Viejo students have ever won ribbons at the event.

◊ The program has been covered by local media and internal (Gowan and Crane) reporting; this has started to increase awareness among the public and key stakeholders of the district's interest in serving the needs of children at grade level and beyond, and of Gowan's commitment to local schools.

Next steps

Based on all the results of this program to date, both Gowan and Crane have committed to continuing the program at Rancho Viejo Elementary School, which will involves an additional investment by Gowan of $40,000 for maintenance, additional software, and field trips. In addition, the partners are expanding GAP to both middle schools in the district at an additional cost of $300,000, which Gowan has already agreed to underwrite.

GAP Budget - Pilot Project

Salaries and Benefits

Teacher stipends (3 @$10,000)	$30,000
Professional development	6,000
Benefits	6,368

Class Travel

Local field trips (10/class @$250)	$7,500
Out of town field trips (2/class @$2000)	12,000
Summer/extended day transportation	$7,200

Supplies and Curriculum

Consumable Supplies ($2,000/class)	$6,000
Reading - Great Books/Novels	5,000
Math - Accelerated Math Program	2,000
Social Studies	10,000
Science - Equipment and Software	10,000
Assessment Program	38,000

Consulting Services

Consultant/Resident expert fees	$20,000

Equipment

Laptop Computers (1/student @$1,500)	$140,000
Network Printers (1/class @$1,500)	4,500
Server and Wireless Access Points	15,000
3 Portable Recharging Computer Carts	4,500
Video Projection Equip. (1/class @$2,000)	6,000
Video Editing Software (1/class @$150)	450
Digital Video Camera (1/class @$850)	2,550

Total Cost, GAP Pilot Project	**$333,068**

The Nonprofit Internship Experience

There are few organizations in education that focus solely on creating and managing large-scale partnership initiatives; Education Partnerships, Inc., does just that on behalf of a handful of large corporate and foundation clients. Best known for the Principal's Partnership, an initiative underwritten by the Union Pacific Foundation, this nonprofit firm recently completed a pilot placing high school interns at nonprofit organizations on behalf of the Pacific Life Foundation.

The two began talking about a nonprofit internship initiative after Pacific Life Foundation representatives attended a presentation on the Principal's Partnership last year at a Conference Board event on corporate social responsibility. PLF had been thinking about connecting schools and nonprofit organizations within local service areas, and explored the idea of creating a high school-level internship program with EPI. There were three conditions on the project: it had to be turnkey, it had to happen quickly, and it had to be accompanied by a strong evaluation component to ensure that the project achieved positive outcomes for students and nonprofits alike.

Goals

As PLF and EPI began to flesh out the program, they decided to build an initiative that would achieve the following objectives:

◊ To provide students with a real-world work experience in which they must apply fundamental academic and interpersonal skills to be successful.

◊ To link academic program content with the workplace.

◊ To motivate students to develop a strong work ethic, achievement orientation, and client/customer focus.

While these goals were specific to student benefits, the program would also have to provide benefits to its community-based nonprofit partners, with

students making real contributions to their work.

The Program

After the project was commissioned in November 2009, EPI faced two challenges: to create and flesh out the structure of this service program while establishing the community and education connections needed to begin implement the plan in the next semester.

They began by working with PLF to select Orange County, California as their pilot site, partly due to the foundation's presence in the market and its relationships with many of the nonprofit organizations in the community–relationships that would become helpful as EPI built its list of nonprofit organizations willing to host an intern.

Once the target market had been selected, the firm established a local presence by retaining a local program coordinator, who would identify

---

Nonprofit Internship Experience

Where:
Orange County, CA

Partner(s):
Pacific Life Foundation; Education Partnerships, Inc.; University and Woodbridge High Schools in Irvine USD; 32 local Orange County nonprofit agencies

Challenge:
Support nonprofits in the community while providing area high school students with real-world work experience

Solution:
Connect the two with a summer work program, supported by significant pre-internship training

Partner Roles:
EPI created and facilitated the program, with teachers preparing students for summer internships and nonprofits providing work opportunities for them

Outcomes:
Students, educators, and nonprofit leaders were all highly satisfied with the program. Students gained significant work experience; educators saw an increase in self-efficacy and capability among students; and nonprofits benefited from the efforts of these interns

---

and develop a district partner and oversee the program's execution. They began to work with Rupert Asuncion, a retired Stockton, CA high school principal and district administrator who had been involved in the state's professional community for more than 30 years.

A relationship was soon developed with the Irvine Unified School District, and two high schools–University and Woodbridge–soon agreed to participate in the program by making internship opportunities available to students applying to the program and allowing teachers to participate as teacher-advisors, who not only would teach the pre-internship course but would also work with the nonprofit agencies where the students would have their internship experiences.

Students were encouraged to apply for the program, and between the two participating high schools, 125 student applied for 32 total spots. Once selected through an application review and followup interviews, the 32 participants prepared for their summer internships by completing an in-school course taught by the selected teacher-advisors. This instructional series prepared them to be successful in a contemporary work environment by focusing on attention to workplace behavior and norms, the employee-employer relationship, interpersonal communication and relationships, cooperation and teamwork, workplace ethics and legal issues, and other relevant topics recommended by the non-profit partners. The training made frequent use of speakers from area non-profits and relied on simulated workplace experiences.

Students also participated in a series of "pre-internships" within the school or immediate community. These pre-internships allowed students to practice workplace skills under the supervision of an adult mentor and a teacher-supervisor.

By the end of the semester, students were judged to be ready for their paid workplace internships and placed with area non-profit partners. Their roles varied by the needs of each organization, but each student took on real responsibilities and counted on to perform accordingly. Some ran fundraisers; some worked with agency customers; some helped with

communications, including creating websites and connecting their nonprofits to the world of social media.

Students were supervised by a worksite supervisor/mentor and maintained contact with their school-based internship coordinator. As part of the pilot, all students continued to participate in regularly scheduled class-seminar sessions in order to debrief their work experiences, receive coaching and direct instruction in necessary skills and learn additional, increasingly sophisticated workplace adjustment skills. Students also submitted weekly logs, and participated in an exit interview at the end of the internship.

Outcomes

EPI collected a great deal of data throughout the course of the pilot, including observation, collection of materials such as coursework and weekly logs, and interviews with students, nonprofit leaders, and educators involved in the program. They saw highly positive results from all participating groups.

Students were uniformly enthusiastic about the program. Because students were given real responsibilities and were prepared to live up to the challenges they were presented, EPI saw a significant boost in self-efficacy; they also saw a rise in interest among students in working for nonprofits in the future. Teachers also saw changes in the confidence and abilities of students who participated.

Nonprofits were similarly enthusiastic, impressed by the caliber of participating students and satisfied with the results of their work. Notably, all of the participating nonprofits asked to have interns again next year.

Resource Links

Education Partnerships, Inc.
www.educationpartnerships.org/

Principal's Partnership
www.principalspartnership.com/

Pacific Life Foundation
www.pacificlife.com/About+Pacific+Life/Foundation+or+Community

The LEAD Program

Sometimes, all it takes is one person with an idea to launch a successful community/school initiative. That was certainly the case in Waco, TX, where a businessperson with a longstanding commitment to the local schools started mentoring in a local high school and turned that experience into the Leadership, Education, and Development (LEAD) program, now run by the Greater Waco Chamber of Commerce and supported by Waco Independent School District.

Origin of the LEAD program

As an urban district, Waco Independent School District covers most of downtown Waco and serves a high-poverty, high-minority population. It is the largest district in the Waco area, larger than all six surrounding suburban districts combined.

The Greater Waco Chamber of Commerce has long been active in the district, having launched their first initiative–an adopt-a-school program–in 1985, shortly after the publication of *A Nation At Risk*. The program was founded by Bill Nesbitt, president of Central National Bank (an independent bank located in Waco), and is now run by Waco ISD. Mr. Nesbitt has continued to serve as an advocate and supporter of area schools.

Following in his father's footsteps, Joe Nesbitt, working at the bank as Vice President of Real Estate and Commercial Lending, has made a similar commitment to education, including launching the LEAD program. The idea for the program came to him after mentoring a group of students from Waco High School: he saw the impact that a relationship with a business leader had on the students with whom he worked, including seeing some of his students pursue and receive scholarships and seeing some join the bank as productive, professional, and well-regarded summer employees. With those results in mind, he wanted to make that kind of experience possible for other Waco ISD students.

At that time, the chamber was already supporting three education initiatives. They still promoted the original adopt-a-school program (now managed by the district) and had two of their own: Business Leadership in Schools, a career awareness initiative involving local business leaders making presentations to students, and Career Start Day, a half-day program held two times per year that brought students into local businesses to explore area industries and careers.

As an active chamber member, familiar with its commitment to area schools, Mr. Nesbitt presented them with the idea for the LEAD program. Given the initial impact of the program, and the fact that this longer-term mentoring model offered a new option for its members and fit with its focus on workforce preparedness, the chamber agreed to host this new program.

How the LEAD program was designed

In designing the program, Mr. Nesbitt continued

The LEAD Program

Where:
Waco, TX

Partner(s):
Greater Waco Chamber; Waco ISD; individual businesspeople serving as mentors; area businesses serving as meeting hosts

Challenge:
Provide high school students in a large urban district with opportunities to explore local careers and industries and establish a career path based on their interests and talents

Solution:
Match local business leaders with students in a long-term professional mentoring relationship; provide opportunities to explore jobs at area businesses

Partner Roles:
Local business leaders are asked to commit to three-year terms as mentors; are businesses are asked to host tours and meetings for students. The school district supports the program by identifying students and recognizing partners.

Outcomes:
100% of the initial class of seniors graduated and went on to college; informal surveys indicate significant impact on the thinking and self-concept of students

---

his emphasis on professional mentoring: he wanted kids to learn how to get into business, learn to be professionals, illustrate the need for postsecondary education, and help them set and pursue educational and professional objectives. And, as a benefit of the exposure they would receive through the program, he wanted students to have an opportunity to begin building their own network of contacts in the business community.

To accomplish these goals, the program continued its emphasis on building long-term professional mentoring relationships between local business leaders and high school students, with a required three-year commitment from prospective mentors. These mentors are expected to meet with their group of 2-4 students twice monthly during the school year, with some of those meetings taking place with the entire group of LEAD participants for tours and discussions at area business locations.

These regular small-group and program-wide meetings educate and expose students to the various business fields and applications that businesses are successful at doing. This is expected to improve students' knowledge and skills base, help them identify a career track, and motivate them to graduate and pursue the steps needed (including postsecondary education) to enter and succeed in their desired career and/or industry.

According to Kay Metz, Director of Development and Community Partnerships with Waco ISD, "These are experiences our kids simply would not have otherwise. We have kids who haven't had a working member of their family for two or three generations, so this vision in their minds of somebody getting up, getting ready and going to work every morning is just not there, and that exposure is what we are wanting to give them. Unless a student can visualize something like this, they don't know how to reach for it."

Finding and matching participants

A great deal of work goes into selecting mentors and students for the program. Leaders in the business community are identified and sought out, often by Mr. Nesbitt himself, to participate in the program. Mentors must pass background checks in order to participate.

Student recruitment begins with liaisons at each high school, often a school counselor or vice principal. These school employees identify students who may be a good fit for the program and ask whether they'd be interested in participating; this allows students to self-select into the program, increasing the level of interest and commitment among participants.

According to Sarah Collins, manager of the LEAD program for the chamber, "It's important to note that students chosen for the program are not always those at the top of their class, nor are they the ones needing the most intervention. Often they're the ones right in the middle, the ones who–with a little help–could really go in the right direction."

Once mentors and students have been identified, LEAD program facilitators make an initial match based on student aspirations; after that, a face-to-face meeting is arranged to confirm a good fit.

Because meeting sites are an important element of the program, program leaders actively solicit businesses in the area to host meetings, with other chamber and district officials supplementing the effort. Businesses like the M&M/Mars plant in Waco have been enthusiastic in their support for the program, hosting tours and meetings for students and mentors. Given the program's focus on postsecondary learning, local colleges and universities have also been pleased to host LEAD participants. In all of these efforts, relationships developed through the original adopt-a-school program have been helpful in establishing relationships for the LEAD program.

Growth of the program

Since its founding three years ago, the program has grown: it now serves 75 students, and chamber leaders have been working to build infrastructure and formalize key elements of the program.

Resource Links

LEAD Program - Greater Waco Chamber of Commerce
www.wacochamber.com/lead.php

One recent development was the hiring of Sarah Collins to support the program. As a former member of the district's Partners in Education team, Sarah works with all stakeholders and provides support as needed. Other chamber staff members, and partnership leaders at the district, are active in recruiting mentors, students, and sites for tours and meetings.

Next steps for program development include adding a community service component to the program, allowing students to take a leadership role in their own neighborhoods, and instituting some formal quantitative measures to benchmark performance along with pre/post surveys for all participants.

Outcomes

As a young program, LEAD relies on less formal data to gauge progress (and is currently instituting other measures as mentioned above). Based on feedback from mentors, students, and host sites alike, the program is making a significant impact already.

One measure of success is that two groups of seniors have graduated from the program, and every single one went to college. For students in the program now, area businesses have created a strong incentive by funding a $20,000 scholarship for one program graduate each year.

There are also a number of individual success stories. One involves a student who participated in a LEAD tour of Hillcrest Hospital's phlebotomy lab; after expressing real interest in the operation of the lab, he was invited by the head of the lab to join them as a summer intern. Other students have found similar opportunities thanks to the program.

The district has also benefited from the program: Kay Metz notes that, by meeting Waco ISD students firsthand, "our local business leaders are realizing that these urban kids are smart, professional, and have a real desire to achieve something with their lives. They blow all of those stigmas out of the water, and that opens the door to greater support and additional partnership opportunities in the future."

NJ Chamber of Commerce Foundation

As our feature story indicates, chambers of commerce have played an active role in education for hundreds of years, and continue today as an active force in the field. One of the most active chambers in K-12 education has been the New Jersey Chamber of Commerce which, through its foundation, has helped shape the education conversation in the state and made great strides in providing schools and the public with the information and resources they need to move forward.

Background

In 1995, the New Jersey Chamber of Commerce's board of directors decided to significantly increase their focus on workforce issues, and decided to establish a nonprofit foundation with that as its charge. Dana Egreczky was brought in to help launch the foundation after working at the Morris County Chamber of Commerce; she continues to serve as Executive Director of the foundation, as well as working as Senior Vice President of Workforce Development for the chamber itself. (Egreczky is also currently serving as Interim President while a search for a new president is underway.)

The chamber understood the importance of K-12 education within the context of workforce preparedness discussions, since the K-12 system serves as a pipeline for future workers. The foundation therefore made it its mission to help ensure that students graduate well-prepared for citizenship, college, and work.

The creation of the chamber's foundation was well-timed: It happened just as the governor at the time, Governor Whitman, had started working with Art Ryan, CEO of Prudential Insurance, through an initiative of the National Governors Association. One of their initiatives was to establish a business summit on education and, with the help of the chamber, it was an extensively planned event, created with all of the resources of Prudential behind it. Out of that summit came the launch of

the Business Coalition for Educational Excellence (BCEE), which was housed within the chamber's new foundation.

This new entity was created with an extensive to-do list in hand: it was given 27 goals and objectives to be completed within a two year period. These were significant goals: one was to pull together a committee of experts on the use of databases from some of the top companies in New Jersey. These experts were asked to work as pro bono advisors to the state department of education, which was working on the launch of its first real student-level database. In another case, schools were behind the curve at the time on the use of technology in schools, so they established a program called Tech Corps New Jersey, which provided businesspeople who would go into schools to help them get their technology systems up and running. Out of the initial list of 27 goals and objectives, BCEE completed 25 within the desired two year window.

NJ Chamber Foundation

Where:
New Jersey

Partner(s):
Varies by initiative, but includes support of NJ Department of Education, Rutgers University, political leaders, and business leaders who underwrite and support their work

Challenge:
Improve workforce preparedness outcomes in New Jersey

Solution:
A multitude of initiatives, including awareness and outreach among the public, business, and education communities; regulatory advocacy; and creation of programs including KnowYourSchoolsNJ.org, an online school performance database; MATHNext, a math-focused professional development initiative; and LearnDoEarn, a program to help students prepare for life after high school

Partner Roles:
Varies; includes support for foundation or full partnerships on development and delivery of resources

Outcomes:
Significant public and regulatory achievements; proven impacts with their various products

---

Since then, under various governors, the chamber foundation has held additional summits, each providing a new set of goals and objectives. One of the larger-scale objectives that came out of a 2004 summit on high school reform was to ensure that the graduation mandates for high school were changed and increased. They successfully met that goal within two years, thanks to an extensive campaign with significant public exposure. As a result, the State Board of Education passed a mandate that students take a much more rigorous course load than ever before. They expect a new set of goals and objectives soon: the foundation is currently laying the groundwork for a new summit, likely held in fall of 2011, and possibly looking at a legislative, rather than regulatory, agenda.

According to Dana Egreczky, "the foundation is completely driven by the needs and interests of the New Jersey business community. They have called for significant reform, so the foundation is empowered to tackle major issues and enact major programs. It comes down to board leadership and the support of people on the chamber side, including the company who have underwritten our work to date."

Since its founding, the organization has grown in two important ways. First, it has expanded in scope: while still strongly focused on K-12 education, the foundation now also works on issues related to the employment of qualified people with disabilities, as well as on the pending nurse shortage. Second, while they have been successful at getting policies put into place, they have also been successful in establishing programs that get down to the grassroots level to help schools do what they need

Resource Links

New Jersey Chamber of Commerce Foundation
www.njchamber.com/foundation.asp

LearnDoEarn
www.learndoearn.org/lde/index.asp

MATHNext
www.mathnext.org/

KnowYourSchoolsNJ.org
knowyourschoolsnj.org/site/

Business Coalition for Educational Excellence
www.bcee.org/

LearnDoEarn: Sample Messages from Student Presentation Materials

Visible tattoos, or piercings on faces, necks, arms, and hands will limit your employability.

The kinds of dishonesty that can result in termination include lying (which can consist of anything from lying to a manager or lying on a resume), cheating, or plagiarism.

LIAR LIAR

No matter how much money you earn, it's how you spend it that will make you rich or poor.

Do you agree?

Let's learn more.

Many colleges like to admit students who have proven they can handle college material by completing Advance Placement (AP) or International Baccalaureate (IB) course work.

You will need time for those courses in junior and senior year.

to do. They feel it is important to do both - policy can be subverted or go awry, so they feel the need to play a role in helping schools do what they need to do in response to the policy changes.

As a result, the chamber's foundation has created several initiatives to improve public education in New Jersey. Their efforts include the following:

KnowYourSchoolsNJ.org

Several years ago, the foundation was active with an online data project called Just For The Kids, which compiled and displayed data on student and school performance within a school, district, or state. They found it to be very valuable and important in terms of compiling and accessing the kinds of data they wanted to use in our work and share with the public; they are therefore in the process of launching a new online data resource that extends on the value of that initial project.

This new online resource, KnowYourSchoolsNJ.org, was developed in partnership with Massachusetts and New York. Users can select any school they wish, and the site not only gives you data on how well (or poorly) the school is doing, but it also automatically pulls up between 5-15 other records featuring schools with equally or more challenging populations that are performing as well as, or better than, the searched for school. By doing so, it eliminates excuses such as large school size, or the percentage of low-income or ESL students in a school: visitors can point to other schools with similar or greater challenges who are performing better.

While the database engine of this site is fully functional, the "face" of the site is still in development; the foundation hopes to launch it very soon.

MATHNext

For the past several years, the foundation has been working to help teachers and school administrators reconsider how math is being taught and what kids should and should not be doing in good math. This initiative, called MATHNext, is focused at the middle grades (grades 6 - 9) and consists primarily of research-backed workshops that help teachers understand how complex problems, given to students in classrooms where instructional practice is designed to support cognitive demand and emotional risk-taking, results in deeper levels of learning and increased engagement and persistence in learning math. Working with their partners, which include the state Department of Education and Rutgers University, the foundation trains hundreds of teachers each year in effective instruction, and has a growing body of research to back up their efforts.

LearnDoEarn

Egreczky notes that, "When we knew we were going to be pushing for increases in high school graduation mandates, we knew that kids and their parents needed to understand why we were asking for that. LearnDoEarn was created in part to answer questions like, 'Why do I need to take Algebra?'"

LearnDoEarn offers students in grades 6-12 a series of 29 classroom presentations intended to help them understand what they need to do to prepare for life after high school, and to motivate them to work harder. These presentations are backed by an array of support materials, including wall posters, classroom exercises, program credentials, activities, parent videos, and online resources, all of which supplement and reinforce the key messaging of the series.

The foundation has worked to track outcomes from the program, and based on its historical effectiveness, they are now licensing their resources to others across the country. They have already seen successful adoptions in several pilot markets and look for continued growth going forward.

The Future

The foundation has found a great deal of success over their short 15-year history; future plans include continued growth of their current programs, an ongoing concerted effort to track outcomes data, and a full willingness to reach the new objectives laid out for them by chamber leadership and members.

Unum's "Tech Night" Program

The United States has lost literally millions of jobs over the past few years; as a result, most people believe there to be a glut of applicants for every opening. But the high proportion of job seekers to available position hides the fact that there is a great skills "mismatch"—in some industries or career fields, there are not enough applicants with the kinds of skills needed, and as a result companies are actually starved for qualified employees. And, to make it worse, many are seeing the beginning of a great wave of retirements among the baby boomer generation, exacerbating the problem going forward.

The information technology (IT) profession is one of those "starved" fields. According to the Bureau of Labor Statistics, employment of computer software engineers is expected to increase by 32% from 2008-2018, with more than 295,000 new jobs created during that period. According to Wanted Analytics, there will be a shortfall of 50,000 workers over the next five years just in the health IT field.

Looking at projections like these, companies like Unum, a Fortune 500 insurance firm, are beginning to take action to increase awareness and interest in the field, and to hopefully secure a pipeline of needed professionals going forward.

Background

According to Andrea Roma, Director of Workforce Planning, Global Business Technology, the need to look for new workers was clear and compelling. "We've been analyzing our current IT workforce and looking five years out for planning purposes. What we found is that 20% of our current workforce will reach retirement age within that time—that's over 200 people in the next five years who could potentially walk out the door. And that's not just us; it's industry-wide. So we're all going to be looking for new talent, and we have to start now. "

Based on this analysis, human resource professionals at Unum began looking at the pipeline for new talent, and realized that there

were some significant challenges: While the level of workers looking at retirement was increasing, the number of people going into IT majors was actually decreasing. And the problem, it seemed, was originating at the high school level. To learn more about the K-12 landscape and find a way to build a bridge from high school to the IT profession, Roma and others started meeting with local administrators and educators.

According to Jim Smith, VP, Shared Services, Global Business Technology, they quickly uncovered a disconnect in the pipeline. "We were meeting with several local principals and educators, talking about the baby boomers and retirements, and where the next generation of IT workers will come from. What became apparent early in the conversation is that the high schools had stopped all their technology courses because of budget cuts—it's just something they had stopped addressing. And we realized that all of the companies that needed IT workers,

---

Unum's "Tech Night" Program

Where:
Chattanooga, TN and other Unum locations

Organization:
Unum Corporation, a Fortune 500 insurance company; local schools and districts

Challenge:
The IT workforce is aging, and as they retire there is a lack of skilled workers to replace them, not to mention to keep up with the growth of the field. This is due not only to a lack of training in IT, but also more directly to a lack of awareness of the profession as an attractive career

Solution:
Hold Tech Night events at area high schools, giving students opportunities to learn about the diverse IT field and experience firsthand some of the challenges and rewards of solving the kinds of problems that professionals face

Partnership:
Local schools host the events and encourage participation

Outcomes:
While still a young program, Tech Night directors have seen greatly increased levels of student awareness and interest, and expect to see an impact through ongoing surveys

---

not just Unum but all companies, were looking for new people, and these new people weren't getting any exposure or encouragement through the high schools."

Part of the problem, they realized, was that educators weren't aware of local opportunities, and therefore didn't have a compelling reason to introduce students to fields like IT. According to Smith, "One of the principals noted that they had no idea what went on behind the walls of Unum. And we started to think about that, and realized well of course they don't—how would they? And we decided, maybe we had better start showing them."

And the idea for Tech Night was born.

Tech Night

Companies can build their pipelines within the K-12 environment in several ways, such as funding instruction, sponsoring extracurricular activities, or supporting professional development. Unum decided that the greatest return on their investment would be in increasing awareness of the career: Students were receiving some of the core skills through classes like science, math, and web development, but they weren't being told how they could apply those skills in the corporate world. And that was where Unum could best leverage its resources, particularly current employees who shared a passion for their work.

While Unum had been involved in some other K-12 initiatives, such as supporting a Girls Inc. technology camp, Tech Night was the company's first major individual effort. And while it has been tweaked over time, it still features the same core elements intended to introduce students to the IT field:

Technology Fair

Tech Night begins with a Technology Fair that showcases a variety of technologies, disciplines, and roles. As Jim Smith notes, "We have 1200 IT people at Unum, and their roles are really diverse. It's not just sitting in a corner, coding; that's one of the jobs, but it's just one. An application developer is different from someone building servers, and there are interesting and different roles in each function of a company like Unum."

The Technology Fair component is staffed by Unum IT professionals who demonstrate technology and talk with the students about IT careers. The fair also includes an "antiques" table that shows how far technology has advanced in the last 50+ years.

Student Activities

The main focus of Tech Night is on hands-on engagement, giving students an opportunity to experience firsthand the skills, and the excitement, that can be found in IT. Activities include:

◊ **Straw Towers Challenge**—Students are divided into teams and given a set of materials and a deadline for building the best tower.

◊ **Software Design**—Students continue to work in teams to design a software interface using a set of requirements.

◊ **Virtualization**—Students learn about servers and why Unum is taking advantage of virtual server environments. They then develop their own recommendations using real-world scenarios.

Activities are designed to build excitement: In the middle of a challenge to build an interface for an instant messaging unit, for example, they suddenly shut off the building's power, forcing students to adjust to new conditions in order to meet their (unchanged) deadline. Also built into the simulations: the real-world requirement to work with others to accomplish goals.

Outcomes

While the Tech Night program is still young, Roma and Smith have been heartened by the high levels of awareness and enthusiasm they have seen in participating students. Unum has just launched an annual survey for participating students so they can see the impact they may have made through Tech Night.

According to Roma, "Given the needs we and others face, Tech Night would be a huge success if we were able to attract a few new employees, and it would be a victory even if we just saw a small percentage of these students enter the field overall."

The Teachers Warehouse

When she was hired by the Foundation for Oklahoma City Public Schools, former teacher Robyn Hilger was well aware of the needs found within the local school district. But she had no idea that the 3,000 flat pizza boxes she happened to receive from a friend represented the starting point of a program that provides $30,000 each month in free materials to local classrooms.

The Foundation's mission focuses on connecting the resources of the local community to the needs of Oklahoma City Public Schools, a large, urban school district serving 40,000 students, 85% of whom qualify for the free or reduced lunch program. For 25 years, the Foundation has focused on soliciting financial support and managing programs to channel that support in certain ways, such as through innovation grants, scholarships, and a community/school partnership initiative. It has also worked to support the passage of school bond initiatives in an effort to attract additional resources to this high-need district.

While the organization had no plans for a teacher warehouse, Hilger was well aware of the need for resources in the classroom. She notes, "I was a teacher in the school district for eight years. The school district couldn't provide everything that I needed, and my students definitely didn't come to school with everything they needed. It wasn't that their parents bought other things besides buying their school supplies; they were just trying to keep the electricity on."

So when a friend offered her 3,000 flat pizza boxes shortly after she started with the Foundation, she naturally put the word out through two online teacher networks – and the boxes quickly disappeared. "They turned into art portfolios, bulletin board covers, and other things," said Hilger. "And then word got out, and people just started giving us things."

Development of The Teachers Warehouse

This new effort grew quickly and organically, which resulted in a certain level of chaos. The Foundation was not soliciting donations, but as community members found out that Hilger could get materials to classrooms that needed them, they began to just show up with their contributions, or call to let the Foundation know where free materials could be picked up. Members of the Foundation's board also spread the word about the program, and donations continued to accelerate.

At this early stage, the Foundation had no dedicated storage or showroom space: donated goods were placed wherever there was room in the office. Building on the initial success they had had in letting teachers know about the pizza boxes, the Foundation began listing new resources on their

The Teachers Warehouse

Where:
Oklahoma City, OK

Partner(s):
The Foundation for Oklahoma City Public Schools; businesses and nonprofits in the community

Challenge:
Provide resources for classrooms in a high-poverty urban school district

Solution:
Connect individual, corporate, and nonprofit donors to classrooms with specific needs by creating an online clearinghouse for school supplies. This online resource, built from an e-commerce shopping cart, allows the Foundation to track inventory levels, create and review order histories by teacher and school, and produce detailed distribution reports for donors so they know exactly how their donations were allocated.

Partner Roles:
Individual donors are contributing materials for distribution; larger partners, such as Feed the Children and Chesapeake Energy Corporation, are providing donations on a larger scale and receiving detailed reports on how those materials are distributed. Other partners include groups such as the Junior League, whose members volunteer with the program.

Outcomes:
Less than one year old, the Teachers Warehouse is currently distributing close to 300 orders/month with an approximate value of $30,000. The warehouse has also attracted new donors who have become regular Foundation supporters.

website as they came in, taking orders and packaging materials for pickup during office hours.

Once it was decided that The Teachers Warehouse would be a permanent program, Hilger and others began considering how they could structure it so that it could be streamlined, managed, and tracked – in other words, how they could move from the chaos of a startup to the order of an efficient and effective initiative.

Given that the program had only existed for a few months, they were unsure what to expect in terms of volume; for this reason, they opted against committing to a standalone showroom, as programs in other districts had done. Instead, they decided to let teachers continue ordering materials and picking them up at the Foundation's office. But to make the process easier to manage, they set specific times during which teachers could stop by for their orders.

The idea for the model came from a teacher friend of Hilger's, who asked, "Why don't you do it like the food co-op? You order food by a certain point each month and pick it up at a different scheduled point; it happens at the same times every month, and you predict it like clockwork. Sometimes you order and sometimes you don't. What do you think about that?" The model was an ideal fit, since it allowed Foundation staff to dedicate specific times for packing orders and to operate with fewer interruptions in the office.

The next question to be answered: How they could manage incoming materials, orders, packing, and reporting. The answer here came from Melissa Milligan, Communications Coordinator for the Foundation, who had experience building online resources. Rather than just post items to an ever-changing list on the Foundation's website as they came in, Milligan took an online shopping cart program called Comersus and modified it to suit their needs. The system tracks inventory, allows teachers to browse materials and place orders for multiple types of resources at once, and produces

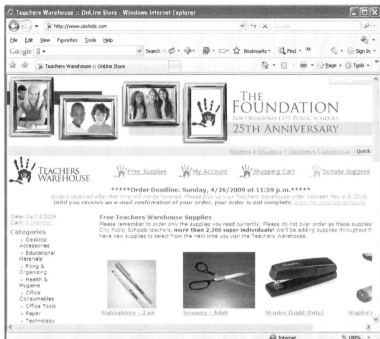

order labels and reports that allow staff to monitor the system and report on activity.

While there is still a flurry of activity around pickup times, chaos has been greatly reduced, and the Foundation is able to accept and allocate a great deal of resources to where they are most needed.

Continued Growth

With a structure in place, The Teachers Warehouse was better prepared for additional growth. And that growth continued to come through donations by individuals, retailers, businesses, and nonprofit organizations. Additional support has come in the form of volunteers: The Teachers Warehouse has been picked up as a project by the Oklahoma City Junior League, and other volunteers, such as retired doctors and teachers, are contributing their time to the program.

While The Teachers Warehouse benefits greatly from individual contributions, the program has attracted larger-scale support as well. Hilger points to Chesapeake Energy Corporation, which is serving this year as the Foundation's annual campaign matching sponsor, with a commitment of up to $100,000. After hearing about The Teachers Warehouse, the utility arranged for the Foundation to take advantage of their purchasing power with Office Depot. Chesapeake had been interested in purchasing and disseminating materials to high-poverty schools but had not found an efficient way to distribute materials to where they were most needed, a challenge neatly solved by the Foundation's program. Feed the Children, another partner, provides palettes of materials to The Teachers Warehouse; the organization already distributes supplies to school sites, but partners with the Foundation as an additional outreach channel.

One of the benefits made possible by the online ordering system is the creation of detailed reports that can be provided to donors. By coding donations with certain SKU numbers, the Foundation can report back to large-scale donors like Chesapeake Energy and Feed the Children with specific information on exactly where contributed materials went.

This online reporting has also allowed Hilger to determine which schools have not participated in the program. Knowing that there are needs throughout the district, she is able to contact schools that have not placed orders to make sure their teachers are aware of the program. While they have not spent any time soliciting donations, they have been active in promoting the program to schools and to teachers, participating in meetings and convocations and getting the word out through other channels.

Because teachers can order every month, there is little incentive to "hoard" supplies, though some items in high demand may have quantity limits. "Teachers love Expo markers, for example," says Hilger, "and we only have a certain number, so they can only order one pack of markers at a time. But because they can order each month, they can order a pack each month if they need to."

Outcomes

After just one year, there are more than 700 teachers registered in the system, and the Foundation is disseminating close to 300 orders each month with an average total monthly value of $30,000.

Melissa Milligan notes that staff members are continually trying to improve the system. "We send

out an email survey to teachers after their first visit and then every few visits thereafter," she says. "They've given us a lot of feedback on the system, and we've acted on that feedback. It's clear that many of them feel a real sense of ownership for the program as a result."

Hilger expects the program to continue to grow, noting that the Foundation has not done any outreach to date to solicit materials. Word of mouth by teachers, board members, and donors, and a number of unsolicited press appearances, has driven activity to date. The Foundation is considering options for increasing storage capacity, and as space is allocated they will work with existing partners, such as the Oklahoma City Chamber of Commerce, and its own resources (such as its email list), to solicit support.

Some might worry that donors contributing to The Teachers Warehouse would be doing so instead of giving to other Foundation programs; Hilger has seen that this is clearly not the case. "This is not replacing support at all," she says. "In fact, it has ramped up support from donors already involved in our other programs." Beyond that, The Teachers Warehouse is attracting support from people who had not previously been involved with the Foundation, and those people are being told of the Foundation's other work and added to its mailing lists, allowing them to develop those individuals into regular supporters.

The Teachers Warehouse was not a planned initiative, and credit is due to the Foundation for Oklahoma City Public Schools for listening to its donors and teachers and identifying the need for this sort of clearinghouse. While many organizations operate from a "top-down" model, allowing the market to demonstrate the need for such an initiative has allowed the Foundation to offer a valuable new program that aligns directly with its mission.

Resource Links

The Foundation for Oklahoma City Public Schools
www.okckids.com

The Teachers Warehouse
www.okckids.com/educators/tw.asp

Houston A+ Challenge Teacher Externships

In an era of increased change in the worlds of both education and business, many businesses are finding that to make their workforce needs known to the K12 community, they must take a more active role in educating local students. Though many opportunities exist for businesses to "go to school" for a day, such efforts lack the long-term commitment necessary to sustain a meaningful relationship between the local business community and schools.

Houston A+ Challenge (A+), an independent public-private organization dedicated to public school reform, recognized students' need to obtain skills relevant to the 21st century workplace. In 2004 A+ joined with the Greater Houston Partnership (GHP), Houston's largest business association, in a week-long teacher externship program to show teachers first-hand the skills local business find the most valuable. The results have been impressive. In 2008 the partnership connected 237 teachers from 18 school districts across the Houston metro area with 72 local businesses to help an estimated total of 35,550 students better understand the demands of today's workplace. Most important, the partnership created an ongoing conversation between local schools and businesses about what students need to know in order to succeed beyond graduation.

Brief history

The Houston A+ Challenge Teacher Externship Program (A+TEP) began in 2003 with six teachers participating in a pilot program at Reagan High School in the Houston Independent School District. A+ designed and implemented the program, which was well received by participating teachers in its first year. After this initial effort, A+ held a joint forum with GHP and the Houston Mayor's Office at which business representatives and education leaders from many of the major school districts discussed the program's tenets with a view towards expansion in the 2004 program year.

Soliciting participants for an expanded A+TEP in 2004 was a collaborative effort. A+ made initial contact with local school districts to solidify interest and participation on the education side while GHP reached out to businesses through letters signed by A+ and GHP, electronic newsletters to members in the GHP database, and GHP website updates to inform its members about the program. The Mayor's Office used the extensive resources and contacts of Mayor Bill White, who himself had been a very active and engaged member of the Houston business community, to reach the business sector and rally public support for the program.

Through innovative public-private partnership and strong communication, A+TEP grew to more than 100 teacher participants in 2006 and hopes to exceed 350 externs for the 2009 extern week.

Houston A+ Challenge Externships

Where:
Houston, Texas

Partner(s):
Houston A+ Challenge; The Greater Houston Partnership; Houston Independent School District; Taking Education to Work; Houston Galveston Area Council; Shell Oil Company

Challenge:
Build stronger connections between local classrooms and businesses to give students the skills necessary for success in college, the work force, and life in the 21st century.

Solution:
A+ Challenge placed 237 teachers from 18 local public schools with 72 local businesses for a week-long job shadowing program. Teachers participated in meaningful team-based projects and developed "real world lessons" in light of their experiences.

Partner Roles:
School districts provided recruitment and administration. A+ provided program organization and execution. Businesses hosted externs and provided financial, technical, and developmental support. Shell Oil underwrote the 2008 Teacher Externship Program.

Outcomes:
Businesses and educators developed a stronger mutual understanding of what students need in order to succeed after graduation, and teachers, particularly those in Academy programs, were better able to convey real-world information on the workforce to their students. To date, an estimated total of 40,500 students were served through the efforts of A+TEP and HGAC.

Project Design

Unlike many other options for businesses to get involved at schools, including teach for a day, principal for a day and tutoring/mentorship, teacher externships offer the unique opportunity for teachers to learn first-hand the challenges their students will face after graduation. Moreover, a full week of work experience provides externs with a level of exposure to today's work environment that may not be realized from a one-day experience. Externships also are unique because ideally, relationships forged between teachers and businesses are established over an extended period of time: A+ calls for teachers to research and connect with business partners before placement (to assure their smooth transition into the work environment), during placement through team-based projects and reflective meetings, and after placement through ongoing reciprocal mentorship.

As part of the A+ Challenge Teacher Externship program, teachers spend a week working on a meaningful team-based project for a local business. On Monday, all program participants attend a breakfast followed by a program orientation. Tuesday through Thursday, teachers report to work as if they were normal employees. On Friday, teachers meet with their business's primary point of contact and review their experiences from the week. Throughout the process, teachers are encouraged to keep a journal and reflect on their experiences to aid in lesson plan development.

Alejandro Morúa, director of partnerships and innovation with A+, believes that to create a successful externship program, organizers must ask, "What are the state's current and emerging workforce needs?" A+ pays careful attention to occupational growth trends in Houston and aligns its partnership assignments with regional economic clusters. Houston is the world energy capital, birthplace of nanotechnology, center for manned space flight, and home of the world's largest medical complex. As a result, A+ has worked with GHP to strategically place externs at industry-leading firms including Shell Oil, Hewett-Packard, Boeing, and the Texas Children's Hospital.

A+TEP admissions are selective; the program accepts only two-thirds of its applicants. Strong relationships with school districts support program recruitment and administration, but sponsors rank and select participants without oversight from local school districts. Participating teachers receive an $800 stipend and continuing education credits.

Components of a successful externship initiative

Morúa argues that maintaining deep and consistent partnerships with local stakeholders is the key to building a successful externship program. He advises that an externship program director must be someone who can work with both business and education, i.e. "speak the language" of both groups. In the case of A+TEP, a skilled and well-connected group of organizers at A+ successfully leveraged their existing business relationships to bring GHP on board with A+TEP. Morúa credits the visibility and credibility of Houston's largest business group with supporting A+'s goal of growing A+TEP to scale.

Effective support on the part of organizers and participating businesses is essential to a successful externship program. Program organizers provide new businesses participants in A+TEP with necessary guidance and direction and often can refer businesses to other sponsors for help. Orientations and webinars held by program sponsors also help new businesses get started with externship implementation. Businesses in turn provide substantial support to externship program sponsors beyond simply hosting externs.

Business support largely comes in three forms:

Financial Support:
◊ Business partners compensate A+ for teacher stipends and absorb a portion of

---

Resource Links

Houston A+ Challenge Teacher Externship Program
www.houstonaplus.org/externship

Greater Houston Partnership
www.houston.org/greater-houston-partnership

Houston Independent School District
www.houstonisd.org

---

costs associated with teacher placement at their sites. For example, a company may pay for extern parking, lunch, materials provided at the site, and transportation to other sites for the week-long activities.

◊ If agreeable to both parties, business partners may voluntarily continue to assist the teachers placed during the following year with special needs for school activities.

Technical support:
◊ GHP members help A+ develop program design and goals to ensure business input into the A+TEP planning process.

◊ Businesses continue to work with A+ to ensure the A+TEP has continual feedback and program evaluation.·

Business Development:
◊ As A+TEP grows, it will need increased support from the business community. GHP has helped A+ expand beyond the GHP business borders. As a result, A+ has reached additional chambers of commerce and has already begun to reach many other business organizations who will participate as the program continues to grow.

Realized outcomes

Workforce readiness is A+TEP's primary goal, and the program's desired outcome is a community of students in Houston ready to succeed in college, career, and life. A+ has identified critical thinking and problem-solving abilities, communications skills, and the ability to work collaboratively as key elements to achieving this outcome. The program requires businesses to provide externs with experiences that work toward that end.

Although A+ is committed to student success in postsecondary education, studies show many Houston students will not attend a four-year college. A+TEP meets the needs of students who

will forego further education in favor of joining the workforce directly out of high school. As one extern notes, "The most important thing I learned [from A+TEP] was that experience and the ability to actually perform the job outweighed the job applicant's level of education, no matter the position."

Ultimately, the outcome of an A+ externship for students is a school lesson relevant to today's workplace. A+ maintains an online database of all teacher lesson plans, which can be accessed at www.houstonaplus.org/externdatabase. Sponsor follow-up visits are being scheduled during the 2008-2009 academic year to allow sponsors to observe teacher externs delivering lessons.

According to A+ Challenge's Web site, the desired outcome for teachers is three-fold: "The experience gives teachers insight into the business world, provides them with new ideas and tools for classroom lessons, and reenergizes them for the school year ahead."

Anecdotal teacher reflections and the numbers of students affected show the partnership's positive effects. As one extern noted, "Business-education partnerships can reduce the training needed by new hires in businesses. Externships are important for Career Academy teachers to ensure that they are preparing students for success in specific careers."

Benefits extend beyond A+TEP's individual efforts. Thirty-three teachers participated in an externship program in Lake Jackson led by the Houston Galveston Area Council (HGAC) modeled after the Houston A+ Challenge. This represents an additional 4,950 students affected by the efforts of A+. As one extern reflected, "The most important thing I learned was the power of effective teamwork." A+TEP shows that with coordinated effort, teacher externships can be an effective solution for creating workforce readiness in public schools.

WorkReady Philadelphia

One of the great concerns of the business community involves the workforce pipeline: employers want to be sure that new entries into the labor pool, whether from the K-12 or postsecondary systems, are prepared for the jobs that await them. In Philadelphia, business and community leaders have begun working together to make sure high school students are exposed to the workplace and have an opportunity to acquire the skills they need to succeed after school.

Origins of WorkReady Philadelphia

Since its founding 10 years ago, the Philadelphia Workforce Investment Board (PWIB) has worked to align the skills of the region's labor force across age levels to meet the needs of employers in the area. PWIB's realized early on that youth - the future workforce - would be a critically important target population, and therefore launched the Youth Council to find ways of improving youth outcomes and workforce preparedness.

As the Youth Council considered options for better preparing Philadelphia youth for the workforce, they acknowledged that schools, particularly urban schools with a high-poverty population could not be expected to create skilled future employees on their own. They explored the growing body of research that suggests that low-income, high-risk teens who have opportunities to gain work experience and to connect education and work during high school are likely to do better in school and earn more throughout their lifetimes. And they realized that opportunities for work and work experience are far less available to youth in urban neighborhoods than to those who live in more affluent suburbs.

The PWIB Youth Council therefore designed a multifaceted program called WorkReady Philadelphia to help area youth, ages 14-21, gain direct exposure to the world of work and develop the skills needed to thrive in the workplace. They enlisted the Philadelphia Youth Network (PYN), an intermediary organization that works with several constituencies in the Philadelphia market, to administer the program on their behalf.

A suite of solutions

WorkReady Philadelphia has several components, each of which utilizes a different approach in order to improve the preparedness of students for the workforce. Some of these involve directly connecting students and employers in the workplace, while others concentrate on developing the infrastructure needed to prepare students, from teacher training to building awareness of careers among the entire targeted population.

WorkReady Philadelphia

Where:
Philadelphia, PA

Partner(s):
Philadelphia Youth Network (PYN), Philadelphia Workforce Investment Board, area employers (for-profit and nonprofit), charities, government agencies

Challenge:
Ensure that urban youth in the Philadelphia area are prepared to enter the local workforce

Solution:
Working with the support of local businesses, foundations, nonprofits and government agencies, PYN manages a stable of academic improvement, career awareness, and workforce readiness programs, operating through a stable of partner agencies to do so. Depending on students' capabilities and needs, these programs may focus primarily on academics; a combination of academics, career/college awareness, and service learning; or primarily on hands-on internship work.

Partner Roles:
PYN receives assistance from the local business community, with more than 100 providing internship opportunities and many more providing funding or participating in programs. It also receives support from area charities, nonprofits, and from government agencies. In terms of implementation, PYN works with dozens of agencies to manage its programs.

Outcomes:
PYN supports close to 9,000 students in the Philadelphia area, and receives high marks from students and employers alike. They also report strong anecdotal data indicating numerous successes.

WorkReady Philadelphia asks its business partners to support workforce development of youth in several ways, including:

◊ Allow area youth to visit businesses in the area and shadow employees as they work

◊ Establish mentorships between employees and teens

◊ Provide internships to teens in the program

◊ Meet current workforce needs by hiring youth for part-time or full-time jobs

◊ Participate in industry pipeline programs by engaging and recruiting future workers

◊ Present at workshops, such as career awareness and job-readiness programs at schools, youth centers, and industry fairs

◊ Provide a financial contribution through the Youth Wage Fund

◊ Support education reform through curriculum and policy development

◊ Provide teacher externships, exposing them to industry trends and expectations through the Educator in the Workplace program

WorkReady Philadelphia runs all of these programs with a $12 million budget, with support coming from public, private and foundation investments. As a result, they are able to place more than 10,000 young people in high-quality programs that incorporate work experience, academic enrichment and college exposure. As an intermediary organization, PYN does not manage this operation single-handedly; instead, it works with dozens of selected local youth serving organizations who operate these programs on their behalf.

The Summer Youth Program

One of the largest-scale programs managed by WorkReady Philadelphia is the Summer Youth Program. The program was launched in 2003, in 2009, the Summer Youth Program worked with 8,800 area youth through their various partner agencies to prepare them in some way for the work world.

PYN places participating students into programs

based on their level of preparedness. Program options include:

◊ **Summer Internships** provide older youth the opportunity to gain work experience, career exposure and learn specialized skills with an employer. Youth are employed for a total of 120 hours - 20 hours per week for six weeks.

◊ **Work Experience** programs combine employment at a non-profit or public sector agency with academic enrichment during the summer.

◊ **Academic Support** programs focus on developing academic skills while providing exposure to higher education and career options.

◊ **Service Learning** program participants work in teams to develop projects that incorporate active community service as well as academic enrichment during the summer.

◊ Participants in WorkReady Philadelphia's **Year-Round** programs, which focus on educational success and workforce development, also complete academic projects over the summer.

Students in each of these programs are required to prepare projects or portfolios that document mastery of academic and 21st Century skills; in some cases, these projects have the potential to earn high school credit. While students involved in internships spend the bulk of their time on-site, even they participate in learning sessions, with an initial training and a weekly full-day session in which they reflect on their experiences and further develop workplace skills.

Resource Links

WorkReady Philadelphia
www.workreadyphila.com

Philadelphia Youth Network
www.pyninc.org

Philadelphia Workforce Investment Board
www.pwib.org

PYN has spent a great deal of time cultivating the business and community relationships needed to offer students such opportunities. According to Melissa Orner, SVP of Communications and Development for PYN, "When we started out in 2003, we didn't have a base of business support; however, because this program was created by the Youth Council of PWIB, we had access to businesspeople and were fortunate that the chair of the Youth Council acted as our local business champion. A few years later, one of our longstanding supporters became chair of the Chamber and made youth preparedness a priority, which helped as well. Since then, we've seen significant growth in support from both business and political leaders in the city."

Orner also notes that, while the economic decline has put pressure on their ability to secure internships and fund programs, they have been able to tap into funds from the federal Stimulus Act, which funded 2,500 youth jobs this year, with an emphasis on 'green' positions.

Outcomes

Despite a very different economic environment from previous years, WorkReady Philadelphia served a large student population, with numbers close to their record set in 2008. Highlights from 2009 include:

◊ Approximate total number of youth participating in WorkReady Programming = 8,800

◊ 109 summer programs offered through 46 youth-serving organizations.

◊ Approximately 1,000 summer internships hosted by more than 120 employers

WorkReady Philadelphia tracks program activity, surveys employers and students on their experiences, and uses anecdotal reporting to gauge the success of its programs. They have received multiple reports of students being hired full-time with employers after a successful internship (either immediately after the program, or after the student completes additional education); they also note a very high percentage of employers renewing their participation each year.

Florida's PASS Program

There are many varieties of partnerships and several ways they may form. Among private partners, there are businesses, institutions of higher education and various forms of private non-profit entities. Schools may also partner with one of the various governmental agencies that are responsible for education, ranging from the United States government down to the local school board. For the past decade, some schools in Florida have experienced a "perfect storm" of collaboration on both fronts through the Partnership to Advance School Success (PASS), a program of the Council for Educational Change (CEC).

At its heart, PASS is an executive mentorship program, focusing on school improvement by starting at the top: teaming local CEOs and school principals to build and execute a school improvement plan backed by public and private financial support. According to Steve Saiontz, CEC Chairman, "First and foremost, the goal of PASS is to raise and sustain student achievement. This happens through the development and empowerment of the Principal's leadership with the help and support of a CEO - and that is the heart and soul of PASS." PASS is based on several best practices involving the use of incentives and rewards, data-driven decision-making, infusing business success strategies, and best use of human capital; all of these flow from the empowerment of the Principal's leadership. It is the catalyst for improving student, educator and school performance.

The evolution of PASS

The PASS program was conceived by the Florida Council of 100, a nonprofit composed of the CEOs of the top 100 businesses in the state. Dr. Elaine Liftin, CEC's current President and Executive Director, with the help of educational expert Dr. John Hansen, worked with the Council of 100 to develop the concept into a working model, with all of the components that make up PASS and the support system to help schools implement and grow their

models successfully. This happened when Dr. Liftin was the President and Executive Director of the South Florida Annenberg Challenge (SFAC).

"PASS is all about business leaders sharing their most valuable currency – what they know and do best – with principals and educational leaders," said former governor Jeb Bush, under whose administration the initiative was founded. "For the first time, CEOs and principals were sitting down and deciding together what their needs were, what the goals should be, and how to get there."

The Florida PASS Program

Where:
Florida (statewide)

Partner(s):
Council for Educational Change (formerly the South Florida Annenberg Challenge), which manages the program it designed with the Florida Council of 100; CEOs of Florida companies; principals of selected Florida schools

Challenge:
Help underperforming schools not currently receiving focused assistance to improve student performance throughout the school

Solution:
Help principals to develop a school improvement plan and enhance their leadership and management skills; ensure that schools have the resources needed to implement their improvement plans by securing financial and resource support from state, private, and district sources

Partner Roles:
The Council for Educational Change, the State of Florida, and the district offices of participating schools provide financial support to allow for the implementation of school improvement plans. CEOs of participating companies also provide financial support, and commit to spending three years working with the principal as a mentor to analyze the current state of the school, craft an improvement plan, and serve as a mentor for the principal as the plan is enacted.

Outcomes:
Since the program was launched, large numbers of PASS schools have improved according to their scores on the Florida Comprehensive Achievement Test (FCAT), with many of these C- and D-ranked schools moving up at least one grade level. Further, many of the schools participating in earlier stages of the program have maintained their improved scores.

Working with Governor Bush and Lieutenant Governor Brogan and Commissioner of Education Gallagher, the Council of 100 developed and implemented "leading edge" policies for improving educational achievement. The Bush/Brogan A+ Plan provided a blueprint for education reform in Florida. In testimony before the House Committee on the Budget, U.S. House of Representatives, Washington, D.C., September 23, 1999, Governor Bush described the A+ plan. "The A+ Plan is built upon the foundation of three fundamental principles," he told the committee. "The first principle is meaningful and undiluted accountability - there must be different consequences between success and failure. The second principle is zero tolerance for failure, and the honesty and the courage to point it out where it exists," he continued. Thirdly, we "zealously believe that our educational system must be child-centered, not system-centered or even school-centered." In other words, the educational universe should revolve around the individual educational needs of each and every child, not the other way around.

The group of Council of 100 members dedicated to developing this program, known as the Task Force to Close the Gap in Education, evolved into the PASS working group, which set two priorities: to support the A+ plan and to develop a program to improve the performance of low performing schools.

PASS in action

With financial and other support of the SFAC, PASS was established as a school improvement plan designed to improve student performance over three years. Florida has a grade system for each of its schools, from A to F; PASS has focused on schools that received a C or D rating according to Florida's standards. The PASS founders did not focus on F schools because those schools were already getting so much attention and resources. Those standards were based on student scores on the Florida Comprehensive Achievement Test (FCAT) and have since been expanded to include other indicators. The goal was to move selected schools to a B or an A grade.

The PASS program gets businesses directly involved in school improvement. Each participating business offers $100,000 over three years, with matching funding from SFAC. The school district in which the school was located agrees to contribute through repositioning and matching resources. In addition, CEOs commit to mentoring the school's principal. "For the first time, CEOs and principals were sitting down and deciding together what the needs were, what the goals should be, and how to get there," said Governor Bush.

While each school has its own improvement model, they all have the following elements in common:

◊ Each principal of a PASS school has two supportive colleagues – a CEO with management and leadership experience and a coach with educational change background.

◊ Each PASS school examines its current status, decides where it needs to go, and begins the process of marshalling its resources to move the organization toward its goals.

◊ Each PASS school changes itself as it continues its day-to-day operations, an approach called "reengineering in place" by the business community.

◊ The PASS effort retains the positive attributes already held by the school, the district, the community, and its personnel.

In addition to the school rating a C or D under Florida's standards, PASS officials sought principals who were amenable to change and those whom the school district was willing to support. They also looked for support from teachers, School Advisory Councils, and supervisors.

With these guidelines, the first seven PASS schools were established in September, 1999. With promising results from the first year of partnership, 19 additional schools were chosen to participate over the next three years. In 2002, the Council of 100 and the SFAC decided to institutionalize the PASS Program and transferred control to SFAC, which soon changed its name to the Council for

Educational Change. Currently, there are 80 PASS models at 70 schools (some schools have adopted more than one model). The CEC continues to mobilize public and private resources to effect change in Florida schools.

The PASS model has had an effect on schools throughout Florida. "The use of detailed student performance data to benchmark, chart and monitor student achievement" has been adopted throughout the state, said Dr. Liftin. "This was revolutionary when PASS introduced student performance data systems and analysis to schools, and from PASS, it has spread to become common practice." In addition, a secondary "Executive PASS" has been established, a model similar to PASS but without the formal financial commitment. Executive PASS is in place in 40 schools in Miami-Dade, Orange and Hillsborough Counties.

The CEC offers a number of case studies to illustrate how PASS works. Two of them, West Riverside Elementary in Duval County and Bent Tree Elementary in Miami-Dade, showed significant progress during the partnership. West Riverside went from a D to a B and Bent Tree went from a D to an A.

West Riverside School

West Riverside in Jacksonville was among the first schools chosen for PASS. The partnership involved Kevin Twomey, President of the St. Joe Company, and Principal Frances Gupton. Twomey visited the school several times to observe Gupton at work. After becoming familiar with the principal's workday, Twomey suggested effective ways of delegating her many daily tasks so that she could put more focus on instructional leadership and time in the classroom. "I truly think that the mentoring from the CEO is the most powerful piece of the PASS program," said Gupton.

After straightening out the administrative end, the team began to focus on improving teaching to boost student achievement. "When we began the partnership with St. Joe, we introduced our new logo, 'If We Believe, We Will Achieve,'" said Gupton. "Adopting this logo was the first step in putting the focus on student achievement. Before PASS,

we were all being pulled in too many different directions, with the students ending up on the losing end."

West Riverside implemented a teacher incentive program which focused on a number of aspects of school performance. These included improved attendance, punctuality, written lesson plans aligned to the curriculum and increased time spent on quality instruction. Teachers who met the criteria received $1,000. During the initiative, 23 of the 28 eligible teachers received the bonus.

The addition of data collection to identify and address problems filled out the picture. "It's exciting to see teachers take test data (both standardized and teacher-developed) and use the results to make a difference in their classroom," said Gupton.

Bent Tree Elementary

At Bent Tree Elementary in Miami-Dade, the Principal and CEO put the focus of their PASS partnership on using technology to promote inquiry based instruction. Principal Bart Christie and Armando Codina, CEO of The Codina Group, introduced "Kids Win With Technology," a project designed to improve student performance in reading, writing, and mathematics. In conjunction with school staff, they examined how the Internet could be used to promote learning among students, parents and teachers beyond the boundaries of the classroom. This project incorporated Florida's Goal 3 Standards, which directly address the skills that students must acquire to become effective, successful workers in the 21st century.

The Bent Tree PASS partnership was implemented with the following objectives:

◊ Strengthen inquiry-based teaching and learning through the use of the World Wide Web.

◊ Implement student writing and mathematical projects and post them on individual teacher web pages.

◊ Prepare classroom environments to incorporate technology into the daily learning process.

- ◊ Improve teacher access to the Internet and a variety of educational software.

- ◊ Increase family involvement in the educational program.

- ◊ Enhance community involvement in the school's educational plan.

Each classroom at the school was outfitted with at least two Internet-linked computers for daily student/teacher use. They expanded access to the Codina/Bent Tree Computer Lab. As a result, students and parents were able to access home learning assignments, age-appropriate websites and complete curriculum-based online activities.

They opened the Codina/Bent Tree Computer Lab three evenings a week for families who were unfamiliar with computers or the Internet. Honor students from the local high school offered free tutoring to parents. Student incentives, such as water bottles, school key chains and mouse pads, were provided for those who attended the computer lab in the evenings.

Teachers participated in onsite computer training sessions and maintained portfolios that demonstrated their application of these training sessions. Teachers also developed individual web pages that were linked to the school's web site. Students were assigned regular writing assignments, including computer-generated samples and projects; teachers maintained an Internet portfolio of these activities, which were presented to parents in evening workshops. "Parent response was favorable, and students demonstrated academic gains along with a more positive learning attitude," said Bart Christie.

The community shared in the excitement generated by PASS. Recognition in the Miami Herald and local community magazines as well as the business publication, Florida Trend, has promoted school-wide pride and a continued effort to strive for even further achievements. Over the three-year partnership, Governor Jeb Bush, Florida Education Commissioner Charlie Christ, Secretary of Education Jim Horne, and State Senator Alex Diaz de la Portilla visited Bent Tree Elementary. During the spring of 2002, the Miami-Dade County Commission presented the school with a Proclamation of Bent Tree Elementary Day.

Outcomes to date

In 2006, CEC received the results of an evaluation conducted by the Evaluation Committee under the leadership of Board Member and Evaluation Chair Lynne Wines. The committee considered four important factors when reviewing evaluation data: impact on student achievement, institutionalization of program best practices that contribute to increased achievement, contribution to CEC mission and priorities, and identification of ways to improve, sustain, and scale-up programs.

Evaluators analyzed school performance by looking at the 2006 Florida Comprehensive Achievement Test. The majority of PASS schools started with a C or D by the statewide scale. In addition, the evaluators note, PASS schools are among the most significantly challenged in Florida.

Among all PASS legacy schools, 2000-2003:
- ◊ 22.2% now A
- ◊ 22.2% now B

Of those active schools in the third year of PASS:
- ◊ 43% made an A or B this year

Resource Links

The Council for Educational Change
www.changeeducation.org

The PASS Program
www.changeeducation.com/PASS/

Florida Council of 100
www.fc100.org

The Bush/Brogan A+ Plan (summary by Council of 100)
www.fc100.org/documents/bushbroganreport.pdf

The Bush/Brogan A+ Plan (audio of Jeb Bush speech)
70.166.63.240/podcasts/bush.mp3

The Council has also published a book on PASS, entitled *PASS It On...Make a Difference*. To order, contact:

The Council For Educational Change
3265 Meridian Parkway, Suite 130
Meridian Business Campus
Weston, FL 33331
phone: 1.954.727.9909 toll free: 1.866.268.0250
Fax: 1. 954.727.0990 email: sistywalsh@aol.com

◊ 43% increased one of more letter grades this year

Among active schools in the second year of PASS:
◊ 40% made an A or B this year

◊ 20 % increased one of letter grades this year

Among all active PASS schools:
◊ 41% made an A or B this year

◊ 29% increased one or more letter grade this year

And among active and Legacy Schools combined:
◊ 43% made an A or B this year

◊ 30% increased one or more letter grades this year

"The results achieved through the Council's efforts are impressive," said Daniel K. Aladjem, Principal Research Scientist for the American Institutes for Research. "Especially impressive is the impact [their] work has had on student achievement, school performance, and meeting the needs of school leaders."

In addition to its analysis of school performance, the evaluation team provided a number of "lessons learned" which suggest that the PASS activity is widely applicable. Those lessons learned include the following:

◊ Principals are the catalysts and facilitators of change. An empowered principal links vision and the reality.

◊ Principals must create an environment that supports academic success and helps all stakeholders to understand and support change.

◊ Districts and school leaders statewide can work as a unified force for improvement.

◊ When business, community, and higher education representatives devote time and expertise to school reform efforts, student achievement improves. Their onsite presence and advocacy validates the importance of the partnership.

◊ Teachers working in diverse urban classrooms need intensive and individual professional development for school-wide initiatives to take root. They must be able to apply this training to improving student academic performance.

◊ Innovation must be directly tied to student achievement goals and supported with resources at the school site.

◊ Partnerships are cost-effective and yield a "return on investment" in enhancing student achievement. Findings indicate that the cost per student of implementing an entire project ($73) was about the cost of a few hours of private tutoring.

◊ When principals had discretion, flexible school funding contributed greatly to the success of innovative programs.

◊ No excuses: Whatever the challenges, all schools, including those with high-need populations, can make significant achievement progress when given proper resources and leadership.

As PASS has demonstrated, it is possible to make dramatic gains in school performance by focusing on leadership development with the support of private and public partners.

Calgary's Career Pathways Initiative

Community-school partnerships come in all forms, and they don't just happen in the United States. Sophisticated and effective programs can be found in places as far away as Australia and the United Kingdom. Closer to home, Canada boasts a great deal of partnership activity, as illustrated by Calgary's Career Pathways Pharmacy Technician Retail Certificate (CP-PTR) program. This partnership, which represents the interests and efforts of career and technical educators in public and Catholic schools along with postsecondary and industry representatives, provides a strong example of a workforce preparedness initiative with lessons that can applied in any market, US or otherwise.

Background

Career and Technology Studies, the Canadian counterpart to Career and Technical Education in the US, has been gaining traction for several years. Unlike in the US, all Canadian children receive significant exposure to career-related content, regardless of their post-secondary intentions. And Alberta's curriculum objectives, established for the entire province, encourage career-related exposure for all students, whether students experience a handful of optional courses or pursue a focused course of study through their senior year.

While this provided a supportive environment for a pharmacy technician program leading to certification, it took several years to create the program, primarily due to funding constraints. Key partners, including the Calgary Board of Education, Alberta Education, the Calgary Catholic School District, SAIT Polytechnic, and the business community, all agreed on the need for programs such as this one - but the funding was not available until a grant was uncovered through Alberta Education.

Planning

The core idea of the CP-PTR program was to expose students to the work of pharmacy technicians over a two year period and take them through to certification as part of the successful completion of the course. While it was expected that some students would specifically be pursuing this career, the intention was to use the real-world exposure and certification process as a broader introduction to the health science field. In fact, the program designers found that even students who expected to become physicians or scientists were interested in the course as a way of gaining exposure and experience, and possibly identifying an opportunity for evening and/or summer employment during their education.

The consortium of partners proposed to offer the SAIT Pharmacy Technical Certificate Program to students in grades 11 and 12. The goal was to build a scalable program in which learners moved

---

The Calgary CP-PTR Program

Where:
Calgary, Alberta (Canada)

Partner(s):
Calgary Board of Education, Calgary Catholic School District, Alberta Education, SAIT Polytechnic, business/industry representatives

Challenge:
Build a career pathways program that gave students the academic and practical experience to earn a certification in a health sciences field

Solution:
Working with a grant from the provincial education board, the partners designed a two-year program that combined high school coursework, a five-month certification preparation program, and on-site job experience.

Partner Roles:
The secondary education partners worked with SAIT to combine their respective courses into a two-year program, a process led by an SAIT instructor who had worked in the pharmacy field for several years. Development of the curriculum was supported by business and industry partners.

Outcomes:
Of the 37 students initially accepted to the two-year pilot program, the majority - 30 students - successfully completed the program, earning dual credit between their schools and SAIT Polytechnic and earning their Pharmacy Technician Retail certification. Evaluations of this first cohort and of primary stakeholders point to a very successful program that will likely be continued going forward.

---

smoothly from secondary to post-secondary education, which included giving students dual credit for their work from the schools and from SAIT.

The program objectives focused on both academic and work preparedness objectives, and included the following:

◊ Offer grade 11 and 12 students in both the public and separate (i.e., private; in this case Catholic) school systems the opportunity to complete post-secondary credentialed career training while completing their high school diplomas.

◊ Demonstrate the ability of the three sponsors to develop and deliver a dual credit program.

◊ Address areas of labor market demand for Pharmacy Technicians - Retail in Alberta.

◊ Provide a tangible successful example of a Career Pathways initiative.

The partners decided that the program would consist of the standard five-month SAIT certification course for this field, delivered over a two-year period in the high school environment. It combines high school courses with modified SAIT courses, and includes on-site work experience with a local pharmacy. The prerequisites for the course involved successful completion of a biology course, with no prior career coursework or exposure; students successfully completing the program would not only receive credit for their high school work, but would also gain credit for the SAIT course - and, in addition, their on-site work experience would translate into credit for Work Experience 35.

In the first year of the program, all coursework would take place within a high school environment, with high school teachers working with a SAIT instructor on course delivery. In the second year, courses would be taught at the high schools and at SAIT (including a lab requirement, and the final practicum took place at a partner pharmacy participating in the SAIT diploma program).

The curriculum content was developed by all the key stakeholder groups, with substantial input from pharmacy industry representatives and from individual businesses involved in the partner program.

Three locally-developed courses were developed based on the content of multiple SAIT courses were created and delivered by one SAIT instructor in order to ensure that delivery was consistent and that students had a strong mix of foundational knowledge and some hands-on experience before participating in the on-site work component. The course developer/instructor was a key factor in the success of the program, given his experience as an instructor combined with his experience in the pharmacy business.

In terms of assessment, students were assessed on nine core competencies, and the final mark was pass/fail. Each competency was judged on a three point scale.

Implementation

The program was approved by Alberta Advanced Education and Technology in 2007 and was quickly marketed to students, as the pilot was expected to launch in the fall of that year. In the first cohort, William Aberhart High School saw 41 applicants, and enrolled 23 of the 27 who were considered qualified; St. Francis High School, the Catholic school counterpart, saw 15 applicants and enrolled 14 (all 15 were deemed to be qualified). Of the 37 students initially enrolled, six withdrew from the program after the first year, and a total of 30 graduated from the program after the first complete program cycle.

Outcomes

As a pilot program (and one funded by a grant that specifically required extensive evaluation of outcomes), the results of the program were studied closely to determine effectiveness and find ways to improve the program.

Program designers and key stakeholders were pleased with the results of the program, including the industry and business representatives who assisted in development of the curriculum and who hosted students during their practicum. There was a great deal of enthusiasm for the collaborative efforts of the parties involved and for the greater level of benefits (dual credits, real-world exposure, etc.) they were able to offer students by working together.

Students were similarly enthusiastic, giving the program high marks and expressing not only gratitude for the exposure to heath sciences in general, but also a greater interest in the pharmacy field specifically.

Of course, there were challenges as well: students highlighted the opportunity for improved collaboration and communication among key partners (particularly between their schools and SAIT) and, like the other stakeholders, noted issues with transportation between the various sites.

Students and stakeholders also identified ways of improving the program going forward, including making sure the coursework was rigorous but

achievable; that protocols were in place to allow non-certified individuals to teach the course; and to find a way to build a solid financial model given the course fee requirements of some elements of the program (the pilot grant covered all fees, but will not be an ongoing source of support).

Conclusion

After years of planning and preparation, all parties considered the program to be a success in terms of both process (planning and implementation among various collaborators) and outcomes, and agreed that the program structure could serve as a model for similar programs in other fields. As the program goes forward and the initial grant is exhausted, there is discussion of finding ongoing support from industry to continue the program, given the workforce needs faced by those in the field.

Two Year Financial Report - Budget vs. Actual

| | Year 1: 2007-08 | | Year 1: 2008-09 | | Total | Total | |
	Budget	Spent	Budget	Spent	Budget	Spent	Variance
Project Development							
Project Planning[1]	$16,000	10,914	16,000	35,683	32,000	46,597	(14,597)
Marketing and Promotion[2]	5,000	4,107	0	24,950	5,000	29,057	(24,057)
Travel	4,000	791	1,000	0	5,000	791	4,209
Program Evaluation	10,500	900	10,500	9,110	21,000	10,101	10,990
Subtotal	35,500	16,712	27,500	69,743	63,000	86,455	(23,455)
Curriculum Development							
Curriculum Development[3]	$34,182	11,893	0	0	34,182	11,893	22,289
Subtotal	34,182	11,893	0	0	34,182	11,893	22,289
Program Delivery							
Instruction	$25,814	21,607	60,000	60,596	85,814	82,203	3,611
Texts and Modules	5,000	2,624	5,000	3,808	10,000	6,432	3,568
Supplies	1,000	0	1,000	555	2,000	555	1,445
Photocopying	2,000	1,096	2,000	2,542	4,000	3,638	362
Transportation	8,000	0	8,000	0	8,000	0	8,000
Subtotal	33,814	25,327	76,000	67,501	109,814	92,828	16,986
Total	$103,496	53,932	103,500	137,244	206,996	191,176	15,820
SAIT Overhead (20%)	20,699	10,786	20,700	27,449	41,399	38,235	3,164
Contingency Fund (3%)	3,104	0	3,105	0	6,209	0	6,209
Total Cost	**$127,300**	**64,718**	**127,305**	**164,693**	**254,605**	**229,411**	**25,193**

Footnotes:
[1] *Additional planning and logistics efforts were needed in Year 2*
[2] *Costs in Year 2 primarily reflect recognition efforts for graduating students*
[3] *Curriculum was substantially aided by in-kind contributions*

Rockwell Collins' *Engineering Experiences*

If you've ever wondered how major corporations decide to become involved in K-12 education, or why they focus in certain areas or structure their programs in certain ways, a look at Rockwell Collins' work over the past 20 years will provide great insight.

When it comes to major corporations, Rockwell Collins certainly fits the bill: The company employs approximately 20,000 at its more than 60 locations around the world, and last year posted worldwide sales of $4.7 billion. As a leading firm in the areas of aviation and information technology systems and solutions, this company relies heavily on a well-educated and prepared workforce, particularly in the traditional STEM (science, technology, engineering, and mathematics) fields.

Origins of Rockwell Collins' Work in K-12 Education

While Rockwell Collins has long been involved in science and engineering curricula at the post-secondary level, their initial interests in, and efforts toward, K-12 education arose from a much broader concern about the state of public education. Like many other firms, they were startled by the "A Nation At Risk" report, published in 1983 by the National Commission on Excellence in Education. This report, which stated that "the educational foundations of our society are presently being eroded by a rising tide of mediocrity that threatens our very future as a Nation and a people," served as a call to action for the business community—and Rockwell Collins began looking at the ways in which it might improve outcomes by reaching out to elementary, middle, and high school students.

Beginning in 1988, after much informal discussion and action, the company took an official position on K-12 education with the following philosophy statement:

> *As a company dedicated to the concept of corporate citizenship and community development, Rockwell understands the*

importance of involvement in key sciences and technological development programs in the K-12 age group.

To maintain and reinforce this commitment, Rockwell has undertaken efforts to further develop existing educational programs and research new ones to enhance the company's overall involvement in educational enterprise.

That same year, the organization began to actively develop its strategy toward education. Part of this was handled through internal efforts, such as the company's creation of an Education Committee which was charged with survey Rockwell Collins' employees at its Cedar Rapids, Iowa headquarters

---

Engineering Experiences

Where:
Cedar Rapids, IA and in multiple offices across the country

Partner(s):
Schools and districts across the country, with an emphasis on Iowa; retired employees of Rockwell Collins; independent education organizations such as FIRST, Project Lead The Way, and the National Engineers Week Foundation

Challenge:
Concerns about the STEM preparedness of the workforce, not only among four-year degreed positions (such as engineers) but also among those with two-year degrees and among the general public (including those in non-technical positions, like communications, that still require STEM literacy)

Solution:
Develop a mix of initiatives, some local to the Cedar Rapids headquarter and some suitable for branch locations, that engage students in STEM through hands-on, real-life applications and build career awareness/preparedness

Partner Roles:
Locally, Rockwell Collins partnered with local schools and local institutions to design and manage various initiatives; locally and nationally, partners such as FIRST and Engineers Week provided expertise in establishing local program sites and in placing Rockwell Collins employees as volunteers

Outcomes:
Rockwell Collins has seen anecdotal reports of success from its various local initiatives, both in student outcomes and employee experiences; the company is focusing much more on evaluation going forward

---

to ascertain their views of the local K-12 system; another development came from outside, when a local school approached the company to develop a business/education partnership.

From this foundation, particularly from employee's enthusiasm seen through the internal survey, Rockwell Collins unveiled its first formal education engagement program in 1990. This included establishing pilot programs with three local schools, as well as creating a K-12 Steering Committee made up of three company representatives and three representatives from local schools. These individuals worked together to establish a mission statement, set goals, and oversee the activities of the company's K-12 Program.

The goals, set during the pilot year 1990-91, involved three key areas that are still relevant to the company's efforts today:

◊ Support the effective teaching of the basic K-12 curricula, including (but not limited to) technology, communication skills, math, science, global awareness, employment skills, and creative thinking.

◊ Increase parental support for the education process and programs.

◊ Promote among students great awareness of the "real world" career options and the education and training needed for such options.

1993-1999: The Developmental Years

While Rockwell Collins had put into place many of the foundational elements of their program, they were still in the early stages of their work: they were still only involved in three schools on a pilot basis, programs were focused on general school support, there was no program or office branding in place, and there was no part-time or full-time staff dedicated to the company's work in K-12 education. According to Jenny Becker, Senior Community Relations Specialist, "At that time, it was a fairly informal model: employees chose the schools they wanted to work with, often based on where their own children went to school, and it was focused on what our employees could personally bring to the

schools, in terms of their own interests and talents."

All of that began to change starting in 1993. After wrapping up their three two-year local pilot programs, Rockwell Collins added four more schools to their partnership program. And, while each of the seven participating schools had liaisons that served on the company's K-12 Steering Committee, the K-12 program had expanded, and employees could choose to volunteer at any school.

To support this growth, a part-time volunteer coordinator was hired after Jack Cosgrove, a senior executive with a long-term commitment to education both at the K-12 level and at the college level, heard from community members about the incredible impact that Rockwell employees were making in the schools.

Another development: 1993 saw the first branded initiative, the Educator to Space Program. This program offered teachers astronaut-style training and simulations, along with other space activities developed to promote life-long learning, and aligned closely with the company's growing focus on STEM education.

As Rockwell Collins' work in K-12 education grew, it launched additional programs, such as 1995's A World in Motion initiative, done in collaboration with the Cedar Rapids Community Schools and the Iowa State University Extension. This program, designed as a curriculum supplement, presented a hands-on approach to teaching physical science and principles such as Newton's Laws. But the company also began receiving recognition for its work, such as the K-12 Partnership Program's internal recognition by the Chairman's Team Award (1995), and in 1997, their public recognition (in conjunction with the SPARK mentoring program at Kennedy High School) through the Governor's FINE (First in the Nation in Education) Award.

The scope of the program continued to grow with the addition of other K-12 outreach initiatives such as:

◊ The Workplace Learning Connection (1998), an organization dedicated to facilitating work-based learning for area students

◊ The formation of the Rockwell Collins Retired Volunteers (1998), which continue to be involved in a wide range of K-12 activities

◊ REACT, or the Rockwell Educational Access to Computer Technology Center (1999), which provides refurbished computers from Rockwell and others to schools and non-profit organizations

2000-2007: Focus and Major Partnerships

In 2001, Rockwell Collins spun off from Rockwell International to become an independent company; at that same time, its K-12 program activity expanded through major partnerships that allowed the company to leverage the expertise, resources, and visibility of major partners; the focus of these initiatives also showcase the company's increasing focus on working specifically on STEM initiatives.

Rockwell Collins' first such partnerships in 2001 where with FIRST (both the Robotics and LEGO League initiatives) and Future City, an initiative of the National Engineers Week Committee; both programs were established with local school districts as a way to introduce students to STEM topics through hands-on, real-world applications. In 2002, the company expanded its Engineers Week activities by bringing Zoom zones to community venues and participating in the Introduce a Girl to Engineering initiative.

In addition to supporting the development of an Engineering Tech Academy beginning in 2003, the company further expanded its work with national partners by significantly expanding its work with the FIRST LEGO League (2004) and expending its local role in Engineers Week (2005).

2007 and Beyond: Strategic Focus

Until this point, Rockwell Collins' efforts in K-12 education had expanded organically; in 2007, according to Jenny Becker, "at the request of our leadership, this work was recognized as a business initiative, something significantly more than a corporate volunteer program. We have identified

it as a business imperative that we inspire the next generation of engineers and innovators so that we can continue to grow and thrive as a company."

Part of this revisioning involved branding the company's K-12 program as "Engineering Experiences", a name that ties in all of its activities and reinforces the focus on STEM activities and outcomes.

It also involved a significant amount of strategic planning around desired outcomes. According to Becker: "One of our long-term goals involves boosting our business success by increasing the workforce pipeline. Our goal is to get more students interested in STEM, to the point that they consider a career in engineering or technology. We also find it important to develop more STEM-literate citizens, so there are people who can work with us in finance, or community relations for example. We also have a lot of two-year degreed technicians who work here. So we want to be clear that when we talk about the next generation of workers, it's not just those four-year degreed employees: it's also about those getting two-year degrees who can come here and make a very good living."

"We want to give kids first-hand exposure to how cool STEM can be, and we do that through job shadowing, tours, and internships. We do that so that kids have good information on engineering, and on Rockwell Collins, so they're not making assumptions and we can dismiss those stereotypes about the engineer nerd in a cubicle."

As part of its strategic focus, Rockwell Collins strengthened its relationships with partners like FIRST in order to provide employees in other locations with opportunities to volunteer in ways that align with the company's vision. Becker notes, "Certainly we had pockets of volunteers at offices all

Resource Links

Rockwell Collins Engineering Experiences
www.rockwellcollins.com/about/community/engineering-experiences

US FIRST
www.usfirst.org

National Engineers Week Foundation
www.eweek.org

over the country. But we didn't have any reporting structure or anything formal in place. So we began to formalize our partnerships (with organizations like FIRST and Engineers Week) to offer our employees more structured opportunities to get involved. We needed to do things that offered some visibility while giving us an opportunity to get our volunteers out there. Organizations like FIRST already have visibility and infrastructure in these communities; so if I get a call from a volunteer in California, I can connect them with someone at one of these organizations in their area who will take care of them. And we really like that some of these organizations have a global presence, which gives us an opportunity to expand in the future as well."

Looking Toward the Future

Going forward, Rockwell Collins is particularly interested in expanding their programs beyond the US: as an international company, they have an interest in identifying and promoting STEM awareness and skills wherever they can be found. They are also interested in significantly increasing their work on measurement and evaluation: While they have already begun supporting evaluation work on their programs, they are also keenly interested in employee outcomes, looking not only at employee experiences, but also at the perceptions of new employees, particularly whether they interacted with Rockwell Collins initiatives as a student or community member. And of course they are interested in building on their successes to date: Engineering Experiences is a well-regarded program inside and outside the company, and will continue to serve as a model for other companies wanting to generate the same kinds of benefits as seen by Rockwell Collins in its work.